A SILENT TRAGEDY
Child Abuse in the Community

A
SILENT
TRAGEDY

Child Abuse in the Community

by Peter and Judith DeCourcy

Alfred
PUBLISHING CO., INC

Library of Congress Catalog Card Number: 72-95493
ISBN: 0-88284-005-3 (HARD COVER EDITION)
ISBN: 0-88284-006-1 (PAPERBACK EDITION)

Printed in the United States of America

The only thing necessary for the triumph of
evil is for good men to do nothing.

—EDMUND BURKE,
letter to William Smith, January 9, 1795

Chapters 2 through 13 are case histories of real children and the agonies they have suffered. Fictitious names have been used; the identities of the communities are not revealed, and some redundant and voluminous police, medical, and psychological reports have been condensed or omitted. In all other aspects, these are factual reports.

CONTENTS

A SILENT TRAGEDY
Child Abuse in the Community

Chapter 1 INTRODUCTION

I firmly believe that every parent has in his heart a desire to be a good parent. Some of them get off the track and abuse their children, but this doesn't happen often. A little kind advice from the Judge, a little common sense from the Welfare Worker, and encouragement to seek God's help is all that is needed in most of the cases we see.

—*A judge's comment*

Now that he's four years old he has got in the habit of imitating me, everything I do. We have been living in this little hotel room for two years and it really gets to me, so when I was scrubbing the bathroom and found that he had taken the scouring powder and was trying to scrub the rug in the other room, I really blew up and lost my cool. I don't know how I come to do it, but I started beating on his fingers with the brush, and he was hollering and screaming and I was getting madder and madder, and when I stopped, I found that I had broken all of his fingers and had pulled his fingernails off, some of them.

—*A mother's testimony*

This book is about violence, torture, murder, sexual deviation, and rape. It is about a minority group whose members are regularly humiliated, beaten, mutilated, killed, or sexually abused and who have little effective legal or police protection from these vicious assaults. This book is about our children.

The events described occurred in two communities. One of them is an affluent bedroom suburb in a large metropolitan area. The other is a medium-sized city which is relatively prosperous, free of the rotten core of slums that characterizes most urban areas, and which has a small nonwhite population. Within these communities child abuse is not an isolated phenomenon confined to alienated or underprivileged groups. It is widespread, and the parents who commit these atrocities range from those who are obviously psychotic to others who are seemingly well adjusted and successful.

Both communities have fairly good programs for dealing with juvenile offenders and believe that they have effective systems of protection of children from abusive parents. Unfortunately, most cases involving child abuse or neglect are heard in the secret sanctuaries of juvenile courts, and the results are not made public. Therefore the people in these communities have no real knowledge of the inadequacies of the legal processes which permit incredible offenses to be committed against children, the number of offenses that occur, or the reasons for committing these offenses.

The forces that impel parents to torture, neglect, or abuse their children are exceedingly complex; they include psychological stress, long-established patterns of maladaptive behavior, and social pressures that are often intolerable. The care and management of an infant or a child is a complex, often frustrating, matter. Many people with varying degrees of emotional disorders, inadequate skills, or distaste for marriage and parenthood find themselves trying to cope with a role that is a constant irritant to them. At one time or another they explode and vent their rage by assaulting their children.

As activists in women's liberation organizations delight in telling us, women, especially housewives, are shortchanged by our society. A woman is often forced by social pressures to ignore her own desires and feelings and assume the role of a wife or mother. If she succeeds in this role, she is "good," she is accepted; if she rejects the role, she is "bad," somehow defective.

Marriage is often seen as the ultimate event, the triumph. Unfortunately, the novelties and delights of the first months of marriage soon fade into a routine existence in which financial indebtedness increases, the husband is found to be flawed, and motherhood becomes a trap from which there is no escape except through fantasy.

The constant demands of the infant for its mother's attention prevent the mother from following her previous pattern of activities. She becomes home- and child-centered, while her husband becomes job- or tavern-centered, or hunting-and-fishing-centered. Her social isolation becomes almost complete. She is alone with her child, and her contacts with others, including her husband, become brief or disappointingly superficial.

A young wife who has learned to place a high value on housekeeping skills too often finds that her child appears determined to keep the home in perpetual disorder. It is difficult for her to realize that her child is not rejecting her exhortations and demands, but rather that the child has not reached the level of developmental readiness that would enable him to understand what she wants him to do. As a result, many mothers come to see their children as malicious, evil, little people who possess a full complement of intellectual skills almost from the moment of their birth. A woman discussing a six-months-old daughter may describe her as a "seductive little sex pot." A year-old son may be seen as acting "mean and cruel." Few parents fully understand the intellectual limitations of the infant and child, which causes them to become frustrated and angry when their demands are not met.

While our expectation of women to marry and become good mothers has remained unchanged, many of our living patterns have become less settled in the past few decades. Our society has become increasingly mobile, with families moving from city to city or from neighborhood to neighborhood. Contact with the old web-like clan of grandparents, in-laws, uncles, and cousins has greatly lessened;

families have become starkly simple, nuclear units consisting only of parents and children. The wife often feels alone and alienated, with no one to whom she can turn for guidance, comfort, or assistance when she is experiencing marital or child-rearing problems. Under such circumstances, even the best child, with its demands and aggravating mistakes, can at times seem a monster to its harassed mother—and she can react with sudden, harsh violence.

Being a father troubles many men, especially those who think they are failures in important areas of life. Many such men, who are anxious to be proud of their children, especially their sons, try to relive their lives vicariously in the lives of their children. They can be kind and loving, but they can also be harsh, rigid, and demanding and expect their children to faithfully fulfill many unrealistic expectations. When the children fail, the fathers seldom blame themselves; instead, their children become the focus of their anger and disappointment.

In other instances the first child is seen by the father as an intruder who has disturbed the marriage, someone who competes with the father for the mother's love. The child appears to monopolize the mother's time, conversation, and attention, and soon the father views both the mother and child as boring or irritating. Minor matters become major emergencies, and the father's attitude toward the child becomes one of angry impatience and harsh demands.

The job of being a stepparent is especially difficult. The wicked stepmother is an integral part of our folklore. Many of us, both adults and children, *expect* a stepparent to be bad. Both stepchildren and stepparents get anxious about the new situation and cautiously watch each other for signs of anger or disapproval. Such signs can usually be found if they are expected, and when they are seen, either the stepparent or the stepchild tends to overreact. The child claims that the new parent is "not as nice as my real Daddy used to be," and the stepparent begins to see his new, often unwanted, brood as resentful and unloving.

Many women think the care of their stepchildren is a price they must pay for the privilege of marrying a man they love. After a few months the price may seem too high and they become angry because of the bad bargain they have made. One stepmother expressed this eloquently: "I go out of my skull in that house. Why should I have to raise that other bitch's garbage while she's out on the town living it up every night? I can't stand it anymore."

Stepfathers seldom encounter the boring or irritating trivia associated with housekeeping or child care that fills so much of a stepmother's day. Instead, they are often resentful of their stepchildren for sexual reasons. We live in a culture that is becoming increasingly permissive and relaxed in its sexual attitudes and behavior, but a tremendous number of men are troubled about their sexual adequacy. A man wonders if he really turns his wife on, and how she compares his sexual performance with that of other men she has known. What did they do together? Which of us was best? How big was his penis?

Most men can keep such unwanted thoughts out of their conscious minds most of the time, but many stepfathers find that other men's children become a sort of living, indisputable testimony to the fact that the mother has had other sexual experience. Every parent or stepparent becomes angry at their children on numerous occasions. This natural anger can be tremendously augmented if the child who is the target of the anger is also the imagined symbol of the angry man's sexual inadequacy.

"I know he's a nice little kid, and none of this is his fault. I guess I'm crazy, but somehow when I look at him

I see my wife grunting and groaning, being balled by another man, and loving it. When I feel this way I could kill him," one stepfather said.

All of us—fathers, mothers, stepparents, bachelors, school children, and whores—seem to share a common need to continuously bolster our self-esteem, to constantly find ways to prove to ourselves that we are indeed adequate, competent persons. One way we can demonstrate this adequacy and competence is to show that we are good parents, and this quality of being a good parent is measured by the behavior of our children. In infancy, a "good" child, one of which we can be proud, is often the child who reaches developmental milestones at an early age. We collect merit badges in the form of self-approval if our child is toilet trained, walks, or talks at an earlier age than the children of neighbors, friends, or relatives. If our child is slow in acquiring these skills, we feel somehow disgraced. These feelings of disgrace and failure can easily be projected toward the child. We become angry because the child has let us down, made us look bad, which makes us angry. This anger can lead to neglect or violence.

Such pressures can become overwhelming even to intelligent, relatively stable men and women; unfortunately a very large number of parents cannot be so described. The best estimates indicate that 10 percent of our population is sufficiently disturbed to need psychiatric care at one time or another in their lives. The incidence of alcoholism is high, and some members of the first generation that turned to the large-scale use of drugs have now become parents. Hence, in addition to ordinary, normal people, we also find parents who are psychotic, neurotic, drunk, or under the influence of drugs attempting to cope with the stress-filled role of a parent; their reactions to their children's annoying behavior are often quick and brutal. In other instances the child and its needs are ignored by these disturbed individuals; real physical or psychological damage is caused by the continuing neglect.

Unfortunately, anyone can become a parent. No questions are asked. In other areas of life, ability, competence, and integrity are not taken for granted. People are investigated regularly. When they apply for a job, they are often tested, their references are checked, their honesty and emotional stability are questioned. If they appear to be stupid, incompetent, undependable, or insane, they are not hired. When a man and a woman plan to marry, they are tested for venereal disease. If they seek passports, they must prove citizenship. If they drive, they are tested and licensed. If they ask for credit, they are carefully screened. But no investigations are made before an adult becomes a parent. Our society assumes parental love and competence, and unless some untoward event occurs, this assumption is not challenged. It is as if we believe that any woman will naturally be a loving mother and any man a good father. Obviously, this is not always true.

In many ways we do not think of children as people with the rights and privileges of adults. Physical punishment and psychological harassment are considered acceptable methods of controlling a child. Children are often punished by their parents in a variety of unusual and ingenious ways that would not be tolerated in the most backward adult prison, and the parents are not subjected to social censure or legal interference. It is as if children were objects, bits of property belonging to the parents, to be used in any way the parent sees fit. Unless extreme neglect or abuse can be proved, the law seldom interferes. However, neglect and abuse, in the form of sexual abuse, violent assaults, and serious neglect, are not socially acceptable. If such cases are reported, legal action may be taken against the parents.

Since the American Academy of Pediatrics symposium

on child abuse in 1961, physicians, social workers, and teachers have become increasingly alert to evidence of the battered child syndrome. Every state has adopted legislation which provides mechanisms for reporting suspected child abuse. These mechanisms change from year to year as state legislatures adopt varying statutes, but as of 1971 over 25 of the 50 states limit the reporting to medical personnel and make no legal provision for reports from others having knowledge of abuse, such as social workers or school teachers. Over 20 states have no statutory penalties if a physician does not report suspected abuse, and in some instances, reporting is mandatory but the physician is not protected against subsequent action by the parents claiming libel. Hence a physician may face an action under civil law which resulted from his compliance with the criminal code.

Such a loose legal framework offers strong encouragement to parents who have injured their children to avoid legal difficulties by the simple expedient of permitting their children's injuries to remain untreated. It also reinforces our national tendency to mind our own business and not to get involved in the affairs of others. Teachers, relatives, friends, or neighbors who know of abuse may fear possible repercussions if they report the matter. It usually requires extreme abuse or neglect before such persons take action.

In many instances parents who have injured a child in a flash of anger are fearful and ashamed when their anger has subsided and they have taken the child to a physician or hospital. They may have a glib, reasonable explanation as to how the injury occurred. In the absence of conflicting information or physical evidence, busy physicians have little cause to doubt the explanation. However, repeated injuries, implausible explanations, the characteristics of the wound, or other clues such as radiologic techniques which offer positive evidence that abuse has occurred, may arouse the physician's suspicions. Then, and usually only then, will the injuries be reported.

State laws usually require that reports of suspected child abuse or neglect be made to the police, the district attorney's office, or to child welfare agencies. When such a report is received, an investigation is made and one of two legal procedures may be followed. If there is clear-cut evidence that the parent or parents have committed an act of murder, assault, battery, or similar crime against their child, they may be prosecuted in the same manner as if the offense had been committed against any other member of the community. But in many instances it is difficult to prove that a parent or both parents committed a *specific* criminal act. It may be possible to show that a child has been injured or neglected while in its parents' care, but impossible to prove exactly how the injury or neglect occurred. In these cases dependency petitions may be prepared which in effect request the juvenile court or other court having jurisdiction to assume responsibility for the child's well-being.

In any case the judge has wide latitude in determining what should be done with the child, as well as virtually unlimited power to enforce his decisions. He may summon psychiatrists, psychologists, or other persons as expert witnesses; he may order the parents to submit to psychiatric or psychological evaluation; he may order the child to be examined; he may make the child a ward of the court; or he may return the child to the exclusive custody of its parents.

As Howard James has so well illustrated, juvenile court judges who hear cases of this type are seldom qualified to perform their diverse functions.* A knowledge of legal

---

*James, *Children in Trouble*, New York: David McKay, 1969.

niceties and the content of appropriate statutes is of little importance compared to a knowledge of behavioral science, a familiarity with the working of the various social agencies in the community, and an understanding of the damage that can be inflicted on a child as a result of an incorrect ruling. Few juvenile court judges have such a well-rounded background.

The National Council of Juvenile Court Judges conducted a survey of juvenile court judges in 1963, with startling results. Of those who participated in the survey (1,564), 27.9 percent had no law degree; 48.1 percent had no undergraduate degree; and only 8.2 percent had an undergraduate major in any of the behavioral sciences such as psychology or sociology.

In the legal profession a judgeship on a juvenile court is not usually considered prestigious or personally rewarding. Aggressive, intelligent attorneys who have judicial or political aspirations seldom seek this office. An occasional juvenile court judge is an intelligent, concerned, dedicated individual, but in the main they are a mixed bag of naive, incompetent, or authoritarian personalities. The juvenile courts have too often become a place of last refuge for amiable politicians who have never really "caught on" with the voters, for tired political hacks who were appointed in payment for past favors, and for legal midgets who have never succeeded in the private practice of the law.

Cases in which neglect or abuse is alleged are essentially an evaluation of the competence of the parents, but the procedures that are followed are similar to those followed when a child is charged with a crime. No jury is empanelled to assist the judge in sorting out the facts; he must depend on his own perception and bias in his search for the truth. The news media are customarily excluded, and the public is seldom made aware of the nature of the cases being heard in the community. In such a situation the most incompetent judge may make the most ludicrous decisions, yet there is no public protest. The public is simply not aware of what is being done to the children in their community.

While these judicial hearings are conducted informally, they are nonetheless adversary proceedings. The testimony and charges involving child neglect are prepared by a member of the staff of the district attorney, often an over-worked, harassed apprentice who is required to present case after case with little opportunity to conduct prehearing conferences with witnesses, police, or the parents. His opponent, the attorney representing the parents, may be a highly competent advocate who, in addition to being well paid, has had ample opportunity to review the case and examine the written testimony of witnesses. He may also have important political affiliations that are not without influence on the judge. The child, for whose benefit this charade is ostensibly staged, is not represented by counsel; there is no one to plead for his safety and welfare, no one to speak eloquently on his behalf.

On frequent occasions psychiatrists—and less often, psychologists—are called as expert witnesses to assist the judge in making his evaluations. These persons may be appointed by the court, selected by the district attorney's office, or hired to testify on behalf of the parents. The burgeoning study of psychiatry and psychology unfortunately is still an inexact science. Expert witnesses in this area frequently offer sincere but conflicting testimony which is often couched in terminology that is incomprehensible or repugnant to the court. Persistent defense attorneys can usually find some psychiatrist or psychologist who will testify favorably as to the competence of the parents. This testimony may be sincere, or the expert may simply say what the attorney pays him to say. These circumstances frequently produce a situation in which the expert testimony merely increases the judge's perplexity.

Despite the often confusing and complex psychiatric testimony, most psychiatrists and psychologists are in agreement that there are certain types of persons who can be charactertized as having "Personality Disorders" and who seldom modify their deeply ingrained patterns of destructive, deviant, or maladaptive behavior. They apparently never learn from experience and are rarely helped by counseling or psychotherapy. These behavior patterns are usually easily recognizable in adolescence or early adulthood. While persons suffering from such disorders are not insane or even neurotic, they stumble through life making gross errors in judgment or engaging in antisocial, aggressive, addictive, or sexually deviant behavior. When they become parents they frequently neglect or abuse their children. But judges are most reluctant to believe that such people are incapable of change; they return children to the custody of parents such as these again and again. Almost all of the children who are returned to homes where abuse has occured are subjected to cruelty as severe as before.

In many cases the judge decides that parents are emotionally disturbed and "sentences" them to a stipulated period of outpatient psychiatric treatment, a procedure of questionable value in changing parental behavior. If psychotherapy is to succeed, the person seeking the therapy must strongly desire to change. This desire must be the product of his own feelings, not a judgment imposed by others. The result of the latter is a confrontation between recalcitrant patient and reluctant therapist, with rare beneficial results.

The judge of a juvenile court is heavily dependent on social agencies such as public welfare departments in implementing his decisions when the parents' custody of the child is restricted. A child may be declared a ward of the court, the parents admonished, and the child returned to the parents' custody under the supervision of a childrens' division of the public welfare department. In other cases, the child may be taken from the parents' custody and jurisdiction given to the public welfare department for foster home placement. In addition, public welfare departments may have group homes, special schools, or other institutions under their control or with which they maintain liaison and in which they place children who have been declared wards of the court.

Public welfare departments are ill equipped for the tasks assigned to them by juvenile court judges. Such departments are understaffed, both quantitatively and qualitatively, because of the demand for the reduction of welfare costs. Caseloads for individual caseworkers are enormous, and few caseworkers have received special training that would qualify them for their duties. New welfare workers often begin with great enthusiasm and elan, which unfortunately is rarely tempered with appropriate education and experience. The usual educational requirement is that applicants have some sort of college degree, but it need not be in sociology, social work, or psychology; it may well be in journalism or business administration. The many new welfare workers who are concerned, dedicated, and intelligent soon become appalled at the conditions under which they are expected to function, and leave to acquire additional education or other employment. Those who remain sometimes have failed in other endeavors and now have found their last, sad, vocational niches in welfare departments. They lack the training or skills to manage the problems with which they are confronted, and few have sufficient initiative to obtain the additional education that should be a prerequisite for their positions.

These overworked, harassed individuals provide marginal supervision of the children entrusted to them. In many cases their attempted relationships with and supervision of parents result in increased parental irritation and abuse of the supposedly protected child. The continually increasing caseload imposed on welfare workers is similar to the action of water being forced into a pipe. If water is forced in one end, it will eventually be discharged at the other. As more and more cases are assigned to welfare workers, eventually more and more cases must be terminated. In desperation and solely to close the cases and lighten the impossibly heavy work load placed on them, many workers petition the courts to terminate wardship and return children to the supervision of parents who have abused their children.

Obviously such systems and institutions cannot provide adequate protection for children. They vary from state to state, within states, and from community to community, but they are universally inadequate. The widespread phenomenon of parental cruelty and neglect has been documented in many statistical reports, but statistics never seem quite real. We can't feel or react to statistics as we would do to the screams of a tortured child.

The chapters that follow are case histories of real children and the agonies they have suffered. Fictitious names have been used; the identities of the communities are not revealed, and some redundant and voluminous police, medical and psychological reports have been condensed or omitted. In all other aspects these are factual reports.

All of the parents described in the case histories were native-born and of northern or western European ancestry. None of the parents or stepparents had less than 10 years of education and several had completed college. Nearly all of the men were employed—some as executives, others in sales or clerical occupations, and others in skilled or semi-skilled trades. Most of the parents attended church fairly regularly and expressed preference for some Christian denomination. In most instances they would appear outwardly to be a representative sample of average, middle class Americans. Both of the communities in which the events occurred are "concerned"—the school systems are better than average; there are many well-kept parks and playgrounds; numerous P.T.A. and women's groups frequently become involved in programs designed to help disadvantaged children.

Within these communities, as elsewhere, children are being subjected to incredible atrocities, here and now, and little is being done to prevent it. This pain and suffering, this bizarre cruelty, need not continue. In the concluding chapter we suggest simple remedial action that could be taken to alleviate these horrors in any community where people become aware of the system and insist that it be changed.

Chapter 2 THE MAXWELLS

Psychologist: At times it seems that you hate these children.

Mr. Maxwell: No, no, you got me all wrong. It's that when I think of their father, that devil Groot. It had to be the work of the Devil that made my wife share her flesh with him, and that makes these kids the work of the Devil. When the Devil is in them, I beat them. I just want to drive the Devil out of them.

Paul Groot was a migrant farm laborer, a migrant criminal, and a migrant drunk. He consistently failed at all three occupations. He served a year in the state penitentiary of a southern state when he was 15 years old after he was caught raping a 12-year-old girl. Subsequently he was arrested at least three times each year for petty thefts, public intoxication, and acts of violence. He customarily spent six months of each year in prisons of one sort or another. He was disliked and distrusted by almost everyone who knew him.

Groot was a rugged, handsome man. Early in 1959 he met Ruth Owens, a pretty, 18-year-old who found him fascinating. Soon after meeting Groot, Ruth was pregnant, and Groot, making a gesture of drunken generosity, married her.

During the next four years they drifted back and forth from one migrant labor camp to another and from one welfare agency to another. Groot was usually drunk and Ruth was usually sick and pregnant. Groot ignored the children and Ruth was often "just too tired" to care for them. Sometime in December 1963 Groot beat Ruth severely in a fit of rage, breaking several of her ribs. She was hospitalized by the police, Groot was arrested, and the welfare authorities persuaded Ruth to divorce him.

Two weeks after she received her divorce Ruth met Carl
Maxwell at a revival meeting. Carl believed in God, a harsh,
vengeful God who would permit no nonsense, no deviation
from the law by his chosen followers. As Carl followed
God, so Ruth came to follow Carl and believe in him and
obey him. Carl agreed to marry Ruth, explaining that he
would be her salvation and the salvation of her children.
She patiently listened and believed as he explained that she
was a sinner and that both she and her children must live
lives of rigid, obedient piety if they were to avoid eternal
damnation.

Carl had difficulty holding a job because he found it impossible to tolerate what he considered the careless blas-
phemy and unrighteousness of his fellow employees. He
was strict and frugal and between jobs was too proud to
accept unemployment compensation. The family moved repeatedly. On August 1, 1969 they came to the attention of
the police.

DEPARTMENT OF PUBLIC SAFETY
BUREAU OF POLICE
Officer's Report

1. Specific Crime	2. Place of Occurrence	3. Case No.
Child Beating	2797 Grace Ct. S.W.	70–1871

4. Date and Time Crime Occurred	5. Date and Time Crime Reported
7/31/69 between 7:30 & 8:00 PM	8/1/69 5:45 PM

6. Victim's Name	7. Person Reporting Crime
See List Below	Ann Mills & Children's and Women's Protective Division

8. Witnesses' Names	9. Suspect(s) Name
Victims	Carl Maxwell (Victim's father) Ruth Maxwell (Victim's mother)

10. Narrative of Crime, Describe Evidence, Summarize Details Not Given Above.
Victims
1. Ruth Maxwell (Groot) db 6/11/59
2. Paul Maxwell (Groot) db 9/29/60
3. Julie Maxwell (Groot) db 12/1/61
4. Michael Maxwell (Groot) db 1/16/63

At approximately 5:45 PM I received a phone call from a Mrs. Ann Mills who stated that she lived at 6644 N. Octavia St and that a girl who appeared to be eight or nine years old had been sitting on the curb in front of her house crying and that a neighbor had gone out and talked to the girl and had brought the girl into the house where she was sitting crying. She would not say who she was and they wished a police officer to come to the home.

Necessary information was given to Radio Div. and a car was dispatched. Julie Maxwell, the girl, was brought to the Children's Place of Detention at approx. 6:30 PM, date, by Officer Ray, Badge #980, Car 7. Julie was very upset, and though she had told Officer Ray her name, she would not tell the truth about her phone number, or address or who her parents were. She stated that she didn't want to ever go home again because her father beat her all the time. She said that she hurt because she had not cleaned the house right last night and her father had whipped her.

Approx. 6:40 PM Mr. Maxwell phoned in. He said he had talked to a lot of people in the police

11. Continuation of Officer's Report

department, and he was tired of being run around and asked if we had his daughter, Julie, in custody. He was advised that we were talking to the girl as a result of a citizen's report. He became very irate and started screaming over the telephone at me and demanded to know why I hadn't told him where his daughter was. He was informed that Julie had given us no information and that we were unable to find out her father's name or where she lived. He was also told that she had only been here in custody for ten minutes. After this he calmed down and stated that he wanted to come down here. He was told that Julie was upset and did not wish to return home and that I would probably call him back after I had a chance to talk further to her.

At this time we raised the girl's dress to inspect her legs and found that there were extensive bruises on her mid-section. These started at approximately her waist and went to about her knees. These bruises were very purple, and some of them appeared to be infected, open sores. We asked Julie what had happened, and she stated that her father had beaten her with a belt the night before, that this happened all the time, that the sores never healed, and that she did not want to go home. At this time a formal statement was taken from Julie which reads as follows:

"My name is Julie Maxwell. The policemen have told me that I do not have to say anything. My name used to be Groot until my dad changed it to Maxwell. My dad is my step-dad. Me and my brother cleaned the house last night, and then we had to go to bed. My dad came home from work after a while and got us kids up. Then we got a talking to and then we got in trouble. We got in trouble because we didn't sweep the stairs right and didn't wash the dishes right. I did wrong and my brother did wrong, but if two do

11. Continuation of Officer's Report

wrong, then everybody gets punished. So dad and
mom got all of us kids up, my two brothers, my sister
and me. We all got a spanking with a belt. Then he
told us that if the house wasn't cleaned up right
this coming weekend, that he wouldn't feed us any
more. A week ago he tied me to the bed with a rope,
but I got loose and he hit me in the nose with his
fist. I don't remember exactly what this was for. A
little more than a week ago he tied me to the bed
another time, and I don't remember what for, but he
hit me with a belt and with the belt buckle. There
are two sores on my right leg between my knee and my
tummy from when he hit me this time. About a week ago
I think he also got me on the floor and put one foot
on my head and another foot on my leg and took the
belt to me. We all got spankings two times a week if
we needed them."

/S/ Julie Maxwell

After this statement was taken Mr. Maxwell was
advised by phone that the girl would be held in
protective custody and that he should be at the
Juvenile Affairs Bureau Monday morning at which time
there would be a hearing about the entire matter. He
asked what the charges were and was told that Julie
was being taken into protective custody due to the
bruises on her legs. He was told that we felt that
these bruises were serious enough that the matter
should be handled by the Juvenile Court. Mr. Maxwell
became very angry and shouted, "You mean to tell me
I can't spank my own children?" He was told that we
did not mean to tell him any such thing, but we felt
that the discipline had been much too severe. At
this time he stated, "Well, I just took my belt off
and beat the devil out of her." At this point Mr.
Maxwell was told to say nothing more, and he was
advised of his rights. He was told that he did not
have to say anything to me, and anything he said

11. Continuation of Officer's Report

could be used against him in court. He was also told
that he could have any attorney, and if he didn't
have the money, an attorney would be appointed for
him. Mr. Maxwell was asked if he understood these
rights, and he stated that he did. He was again
advised to be at the 10 AM hearing, Monday, August 4.

Officer Lucas from Identification Division was
contacted and the girl was taken to Identification
for pictures. Two colored Polaroid pictures were
taken of the bruises on her leg and body. At
approximately 8:15 PM Julie was transported to the
Juvenile Affairs Bureau Wilson Shelter for
Children.

At approximately 8:30 PM Mr. Maxwell phoned again
and demanded to know what he should do to get his
daughter back. We again advised him that there was
nothing he could do until the hearing on Monday
morning. He then asked if it would be all right if he
came into the office to talk about the situation.
He was told that if he wanted to, he certainly could
come. He asked if he would be arrested if he came in
and was told not at this time, but that charges
might be placed against him in the future. He said
he would be down very shortly.

Detectives who were available were contacted
and asked to assist with the interview. At
approximately 9:45 PM Mr. and Mrs. Maxwell and
three children arrived. Mrs. Maxwell was extremely
upset and irrational the whole time she was here.
She screamed at me and the other officers and
attempted to hit one and called us several wild
names. She also threatened to kill us if we tried to
take her children away from her. She finally became
so upset that she was taken into custody and removed
to the psychiatric ward of the County Hospital.

Subsequent to these events Ruth Maxwell bent over
to tie her shoelace and bruises were observed on her

11. Continuation of Officer's Report

leg. Further examination revealed that she had
extensive bruises on the inside of her right thigh
and a few on her buttocks. She stated that these
were inflicted last night by her father. The other
children were then examined and it was discovered
that Paul had extensive bruises on his right thigh
and buttocks which he stated were inflicted last
night by his father. His penis was bruised and the
flesh on the foreskin was scarred and torn. He
attributed this to previous beatings inflicted
upon him by his father. Michael appeared to have
suffered the most serious injuries. He had bruises
and open cuts across his upper and lower back, his
buttocks and both thighs. He had an extremely large
bruise under his scrotum and his penis was cut and
bruised.

The degree of cuts and bruises on these children
was unbelievable, and Identification was again
called and arrangements were made to photograph
these injuries. It was noticed that the children
behaved almost like little soldiers. They were very
well behaved almost to the point of being trained.
When they were asked a question, they replied "yes
ma'am" or "yes sir" immediately. They all said that
they loved their stepfather; however, it is hard to
believe that they know what love means. It was felt
that they had been told to say that they loved their
stepfather rather than having real affection for
him. Julie was the only one who said that she did not
like her stepfather, and she was the one who ran
away. We believe that these children have been
terribly damaged, psychologically as well as
physically and request that a petition be prepared
on all the children so that the parents may not gain
control of them.

Following the examination of the children Mr.
Maxwell was advised that all of the children would

11. Continuation of Officer's Report

be taken into protective custody. He stated that he
believed he was doing his duty as a stepfather by
hitting the children with his belt and that his wife
agreed with his treatment. He then became extremely
agitated and stated that he knew the police
department was interested in persecuting his
family. He made what he termed a "formal" request
that the police take their vengeance on him and
lock him up for the rest of his life or crucify him
rather than taking their vengeance on his wife and
his children. Consideration was given to holding
this man for psychiatric evaluation, but he did
eventually become quiet, left the station, and
returned to his home.

/S/ John H. Turnau
Badge No. 361
1st Nite Relief

10:45 PM 8-1-69

A preliminary hearing was held at 10 a.m., Monday,
August 4, 1969, Referee Alfred Mitchie presiding. Present
were the Maxwell children, Mr. and Mrs. Maxwell, Mr.
Jerry Rusk, attorney for the parents, Mrs. Gardner of the
Welfare Department, Officer Turnau of the Police Depart-
ment, and Mr. Raymond Hazel, Deputy District Attorney.
After reviewing the evidence presented in the case, Referee
Mitchie ruled:

1. Temporary custody of the children was to be given to
the Department of Welfare and the children were to be
placed in the County Hospital for a complete physical and
psychiatric evaluation.
2. The Department of Welfare was ordered to arrange for
supervised visits between the children and the parents.

3. Mr. Maxwell was ordered to receive a psychiatric evaluation from the Mental Health Out Patient Clinic.

4. The County Hospital was ordered to report their findings as to Mrs. Maxwell's mental status.

5. The Juvenile Affairs Bureau and the Police Department were ordered to make an extensive investigation of the Maxwell family.

6. A formal hearing was scheduled for 10 a.m., Tuesday, September 2, 1969.

The case was assigned to the docket of Judge Chester Beshaw, an elderly man with deep religious convictions. He was a member of a fundamentalist sect and had held a variety of lay offices in his congregation. He had acquired a moderate degree of notoriety by his frequent appearances at school board meetings throughout the county to vigorously denounce various academic courses which he termed "Godless."

When the formal hearing was convened, the first witness presented by Mr. Hazel, the Deputy District Attorney, was Jane Grace, M.D., a resident internist at the County Hospital. Dr. Grace testified as to the physical and mental condition of the Maxwell children.

The Maxwell's daughter had cryptogenic epilepsy with a long history of seizures. Mr. Maxwell had opposed any treatment for this condition, advised Dr. Grace that "it was the will of God," and had further expressed the opinion that Ruth would "outgrow it." Dr. Grace testified that Ruth's back, buttocks, and thighs had extensive scar tissue as well as cuts and contusions. She stated that these injuries were compatible with a hypothesis that the girl had been severely beaten over an extended period of time. The psychiatric findings were that Ruth was of normal intelligence, but that she was an extremely shy, inhibited child who was forced to rely on a rich fantasy life for the gratification of her emotional needs. It was suggested that unless her environment was modified, a schizophrenic process might possibly ensue.

Dr. Grace's testimony suggested that neither Paul nor Michael suffered from any physical abnormalities other than scar tissue and evidence of recent trauma which was suggestive of repeated beatings. Like Ruth, they were found to be extremely inhibited, but apparently they had made friends with children of their own age, which enabled them to fulfill many of their emotional needs.

The physical examination of Julie revealed that her tongue was badly scarred and that there were large amounts of scar tissue on the inner mouth. Dr. Grace testified that Mr. Maxwell advised her that these scars were the results of burns caused by Julie's childhood habit of licking electrical outlets. Julie told the doctor that the burns had been caused several years earlier by her father, who put live electric plugs in her mouth. It was also found that Julie had suffered meningitis in infancy, which had caused moderate brain damage. Her present level of intellectual functioning was seen as being in the borderline range of mental retardation. The psychiatric evaluation also indicated that she was not capable of suppressing her desires for immediate gratification of her needs, and that when she was thwarted or frustrated, she tended to develop many explosive tendencies.

Testimony as to Mr. Maxwell's emotional state was given by Samuel Douglas, Ph.D., a psychologist on the staff of the County Mental Health Out-Patient Clinic. He described the various tests and diagnostic tools that had been used and stated that Mr. Maxwell was highly intelligent, but that he was psychotic. He was found to be quite egocentric, authoritarian, and resentful. He believed that he had a special relationship with God and that he was acting as God's agent on earth. He appeared to believe sincerely that the Devil could physically enter the bodies of the children and cause them to misbehave, and that when he beat the children, he was, in fact, beating the Devil and helping the children by driving the Devil, who had possessed them, from their bodies. In view of this delusional thinking, Dr. Douglas expressed the firm opinion that Mr. Maxwell would be a continuing threat to his stepchildren if they remained in his custody. The tentative diagnosis was Schizophrenia, Paranoid Type, and Mr. Maxwell's recovery was highly unlikely.

Testimony on Mrs. Maxwell's mental status was given by Phillip Gossen, M.D., a psychiatric resident at the County Hospital. He stated that Mrs. Maxwell was mentally retarded, with an IQ of 69. It was his opinion that her impaired intellectual functioning, coupled with developmental and environmental factors, had so crippled Mrs. Maxwell's personality that she was unable to react to stress in any adaptive way. She was excitable, emotionally unstable, and attention-seeking. His diagnosis was Hysterical Personality with borderline mental retardation. It was his opinion that little could be done to effect improvement in Mrs. Maxwell's coping mechanisms.

Mrs. Gardner of the Welfare Department offered testimony in which she described her investigation of the Maxwell family. She stated that none of the neighbors had been aware of any unusual events in the Maxwell home, and that the Maxwells were generally regarded as moral, hard-working, desirable neighbors. However, various school personnel reported that the children often appeared exhausted during the school day and that both Ruth and Paul Maxwell had begged their teachers never to send any adverse reports to their father, stating that if he discovered that their behavior and academic achievement was less than excellent, they would be severely punished. She further stated that following the preliminary hearing Mr. and Mrs. Maxwell had made two supervised visits to their children. During these visits the parents were extremely hostile toward the children and condemned them for complaining about receiving punishment that they rightfully deserved. On one occasion Mr. Maxwell told the children that they would all "roast in Hell."

Detective Sgt. Halbert of the Police Department testified that neither Mr. nor Mrs. Maxwell had a criminal record and that neither of them had been arrested or charged with any crime. He further stated that he had been unable to discover any adverse information about the couple in the community except that Mr. Maxwell's fellow employees characterized him as a "religious nut."

The defense attorney, Paul Heiser, presented 23 witnesses, including the pastors of two churches, neighbors, and relatives. These witnesses strongly stated their opinions that the Maxwell children were well clothed, well fed, well housed, and well behaved. Both Mr. and Mrs. Maxwell were described as being frugal, industrious, well behaved, and highly moralistic. Several of the witnesses, including the two pastors, expressed indignation at the notion that Mr. and Mrs. Maxwell were considered anything but highly suitable parents.

The decision of the court was given on September 3, 1969.

STATE CIRCUIT COURT
Juvenile Division

In the Matter of	)	*No. 75,329*
Carl and Ruth Maxwell	)	DISPOSITION AND ORDER
and Minor Children	)	

The above entitled matter having been heard on the *2nd* day of *September 1969,* upon the petition of *Police Department* praying that an investigation be made of the circumstances concerning the above named minors, the following persons being present at the hearing: *Carl and Ruth Maxwell; the Maxwell Children; Paul Heiser, attorney; Deputy District Attorney Raymond Hazel; Welfare Worker Ruth Gardner; witnesses.*

and it appearing to the Court, and the Court finding that:

1. Due notice of this proceeding has been given all persons interested herein.

2. The minor is a citizen of this county and under the jurisdiction of the Court.

The Court being fully advised in the premises:

NOW THEREFORE IT IS HEREBY ADJUDGED AND ORDERED:

Based upon the testimony offered the Court finds that the Maxwells are concerned and competent parents, but that on occasion their concern has resulted in excessive physical punishment.

It is further found that it is in the best interest of the children that they be returned to the custody of their parents, and the parents are ordered to refrain from employing physical punishment as a method of correcting or disciplining their children.

Dated this *3rd* day of *September 1969.*

/S/ *Chester Beshaw*
_____
Judge

Those of us who are not lawyers or judges are astonished at how rapidly their behavior changes when they leave a courtroom. All signs of legal aloofness usually disappear and the anger or irritation displayed in the court is replaced by easy camaraderie. Not so with Judge Beshaw.

After he had given a decision in the Maxwell case and the court was adjourned, Beshaw was extremely angry. He addressed a tirade to Raymond Hazel, the Deputy District Attorney.

"You and the police are getting too nosey," he said. "You're sticking your noses into everything. And those doctors and psychologists—all that stuff they try to pull. I was going to be a doctor until I found I had to study a lot of algebra and physics. Tell me, in God's good name, what does a doctor need with algebra? You might as well know I'll *never* take children away from good, God-fearing people like these Maxwells. You heard what those two preachers said; they knew what they were talking about. The Maxwells are all right. Maybe they just try too hard to do what's right."

On September 23, 1969 Julie Maxwell was found wandering on a city street, badly beaten. She had cuts and bruises about her head and neck, and her jaw was fractured. Her buttocks and thighs were covered with cuts and bruises. She was hospitalized, and when she was able to talk, she was questioned by the police. She appeared to be terrified and incoherent, and refused to say who had beaten her, stating that "if I say my dad did it, he will kill me." No formal charges were placed against Mr. and Mrs. Maxwell because it could not be shown that they were the ones who injured Julie. However, they consented to have Julie placed in a boarding school for retarded children.

No further reports were received about this family until January 7, 1970, when Paul's school reported that he was unable to sit in class because of injuries at the base of his spine. The Juvenile Affairs Bureau took him into protective custody and a physical examination revealed cuts and bruises on his upper and lower back, a large bruise at the base of his spine, cuts and bruises on his inner thighs and genitals. He was extremely frightened and stated over and over, "I don't know what happened. My dad didn't do it."

An informal hearing was held on January 9, with Judge Beshaw again presiding. Mr. and Mrs. Maxwell, their attorney, and a representative of the Juvenile Affairs Bureau were present. Paul refused to say how he had gotten his injuries. Both Mr. and Mrs. Maxwell denied any knowledge of the injuries, claiming that he must have had a fight with another boy. A request by the representative of the Juvenile Affairs Bureau that the other children be placed in their custody and given physical examinations was denied. The judge ruled that since it could not be shown that Mr. or Mrs. Maxwell had abused Paul, no action should be taken.

Mr. and Mrs. Maxwell now have full custody of their children who apparently are so terrorized that they will not testify against their parents. Both the police and the Juvenile Affairs Bureau believe that in view of the attitude of the courts, they are powerless to take effective action. Hence, this extremely deviant couple are at liberty to continue their physical and emotional torture of their children.

Chapter 3 MARTHA NAUCK

> I know it's terrible of me, but I can't help hating my little
> girl. She's so well behaved and everybody says she's such a
> sweet little thing, but sometimes I just want to kill her. She
> doesn't have to do anything. I can just look at her and
> hate her.
>
> —*A mother's comment in psychotherapy*

Martha Nauck began to feel that she must be going crazy.
She was obsessed with hatred of her six-year-old daughter,
Sara. She might be at a party or a movie or doing housework and suddenly she would become aware that she was
enraged and was hoping that Sara would die, run away, or
somehow just disappear. Martha felt very strongly that she
should love the child, and she knew that there was no logical reason for her angry preoccupations, but she found
herself completely unable to rid her mind of her terrible,
frightening feelings.

Martha was 25, beautiful, and married to a man her own
age who was happily employed as comptroller for a small
manufacturer. They had a new home in a new suburb, and
most of their friends thought they were happy and successful.

But Martha did not think so. She was frightened and
unhappy and became sufficiently alarmed to consult her
family physician and hesitantly explain her feelings to him.
He attempted to reassure her and explained that it was
natural enough for a mother to become irritated at her
children and that she certainly was not going crazy. "If
you were really crazy, you wouldn't be here," he said.

He prescribed a mild tranquilizer and at the conclusion
of the 10-minute interview urged Martha to come back if
the medication did not help. Martha faithfully took the

medication, but her feelings of hatred toward the child continued; she began to despise herself for having these feelings. She became increasingly irritable and depressed and finally began seriously to contemplate suicide.

She attempted to discuss her feelings of rage and depression with her husband, Tom. Unfortunately Tom had become increasingly irritated with Martha because of her depression and agitation and was not sympathetic. "Forget it; it's all in your head," he said and laughed at her.

Martha slapped him across the face as hard as she could, then ran into the bathroom and locked the door and cried. She was in complete despair, realizing that if she was capable of hitting her husband, she was also capable of hitting Sara, whom she hated so much. As she sobbed, she realized that she desperately needed someone to help her and decided to find a psychiatrist with whom she could discuss her problems.

This outburst startled Tom; after Martha calmed down, they discussed her feelings and agreed that she should see a psychiatrist. The following week she phoned several psychiatrists picked at random from the telephone directory, but was appalled to find that their fees ranged from $35 to $70 an hour and that none of them would make any commitment as to the length of time that it might be necessary for her to be seen. She discussed this with Tom, and they agreed that they could not afford this type of treatment. It occurred to them that Martha might be able to get help at the local medical school, so she phoned and was given an appointment at the Department of Psychiatry. She was interviewed by a resident psychiatrist and given an extensive battery of psychological tests by an intern in psychology. An appointment was made for the following week.

At her second appointment, Martha was seen by an associate professor of psychiatry who explained to her that the department had a dual function in providing services to the community. The first and primary function was to provide "good teaching experiences" for psychiatric residents. The service to the patient was of secondary importance. He further explained that Martha's symptoms were not uncommon and that she would not be a "good case" for teaching purposes; therefore, they must decline to help her. However, he recommended that she apply for services at the County Mental Health Out-Patient Clinic.

The name of this suggested agency was repugnant to Martha. "County clinic" suggested a low-grade sort of charity, and the term "mental health" reinforced her fears that this was what she lacked and that the psychiatrist at the medical school had indeed thought she was crazy. Nevertheless, she applied to the county agency and four days later was interviewed by a psychiatrist, Dr. Rauch.

Dr. Rauch was a quiet, kindly man who practiced a form of nondirective therapy. Such therapists try to create a permissive atmosphere in which the patient can find the courage to experience and express his own feelings and eventually, through his growing awareness, find adaptive ways of coping with his problems. When Martha arrived for her first session, she was prepared for a question-and-answer type of interview and was somewhat taken aback when Dr. Rauch did not ask questions, but simply indicated that she could talk about anything she cared to discuss.

In her first few sessions Martha confined her comments largely to her hatred of her daughter and her belief that there was something terribly wrong with her if she had such feelings.

As therapy progressed she began to discuss her appearance, her childhood and adolescence. She was aware, on one level, that she was an extremely attractive woman, but on another level she felt that she was an "ugly duckling." She attributed her feelings to her childhood experiences: "I was very tall and awkward when I started to kindergarten, and everyone used to tease me. Other kids always played tricks on me, and my mother continually nagged me about not standing up straight or about not watching where I was going when I stumbled over things. As I remember it, I was very unhappy and it seemed to me when I was a little girl that I was completely different from everybody else." Her situation did not improve as she grew older. "No matter how hard I tried I still believed that I was ugly, awkward, and stupid. When I started high school, lots of boys asked me for dates, but I believed that they were only after one thing—sex. I went out with lots of different boys, but when they began to make passes at me, I would drop them and not go out with them anymore. I was still a virgin when I graduated from high school, but—but—" she blushed and stuttered, "I was a straight A student. That's silly. I know I feel silly about sex, but I guess I felt I couldn't do that right either, and the whole idea of being that close to anyone scared me."

During the next several interviews Martha continued to discuss her feelings toward her daughter, Sara, and the trauma that she, Martha, had experienced in childhood and adolescence. After about six weeks in this vein she moved on to the subject of her husband and their marriage.

I was a sophomore in college when I met Tom. I was playing the role of the intellectual—you know, the whole bit—straight A's, wild causes, contempt for bourgeois society. Tom changed all that. He was a very physical person, always touching or fondling me. He virtually raped me on our third date. It frightened me to discover that I enjoyed it.

Tom's ways of looking at things were very different from my own. He was an enthusiastic business administration major, and he laughed at many of the things that I thought were important. We found we enjoyed sex together, but that was it. We disagreed about everything else. The problems started when I discovered that I was pregnant. I didn't know what to do, so I talked to Tom about it. He was very decent and didn't even ask me if he was the father. It was just assumed that it was his responsibility, and of course, it was. I had never experienced sex with any other man, and I still haven't.

Neither Tom nor I thought that an abortion was a good idea. The only out for us was to get married. Both of our parents were terribly upset when we told them of our plans. They tried to persuade us to wait until we had graduated. The pressure to wait became so intense that we finally had to tell them that I was pregnant. My father cried when I told him that I was going to have a baby. He sat sobbing with his head in his hands telling how I had disappointed him. My mother took it a lot better and became almost happy making plans for the wedding. She was disappointed when Tom and I told her that we were not going to have a big wedding, just a quiet little justice of the peace sort of thing.

Tom's father was worst of all. He was a bricklayer. He had worked hard all his life and was awfully anxious to have Tom finish college and find some profession that would enable him to do something other than work with his hands. He became angry with me. He accused me of ruining his son's life. He was sure Tom would drop out of college—the more he thought about that, the angrier he got. Finally he practically called me a whore. Tom and I walked out while he was still shouting.

We were married, and I worked as long as I could, while Tom got a night job. Somehow we scraped through, and as soon as the baby was born I went back to work. Of course, I had to drop out of school. The big thing was to get Tom his degree so he could get a decent job.

As Martha described the marriage she dwelt at length on her difficulties when Sara was a baby. She worked full time in an office and had a babysitter stay with the child. When she came home, she cleaned the house, washed, prepared meals, and took care of the baby. It was an endless grind.

In succeeding sessions Martha discussed her husband's success, relating how he had worked very hard and had recently been appointed comptroller of his company. For the first time since their marriage they would be able to buy many of the things they wanted and get out of the debt that had plagued them. Following this, Martha began to discuss her life during the past few years.

"I hope when we have enough money to do what we want that I will be able to escape from that damned house. Since we have been married I have never been able to make any friends that were interested in the sort of things that interest me. It seems that my friends have to be the wives of Tom's friends, and when we get together, all we talk about is our husbands and their jobs. That damn company seems to fill our lives 24 hours a day."

Martha became tearful as she discussed her disillusionment with Tom. "He really is just a bookkeeping machine. He doesn't know or care anything about the world in which he lives. All he's interested in is his job. He is getting more and more turned off as far as I am concerned, and our sex life has practically disappeared.

"I'm really ashamed of him. He's just a rigid, straight-laced, middle-class WASP with no imagination and no goal in life except to make more money for himself and for that damned company. I wish I had never got pregnant and had to marry him." She sobbed uncontrollably for several minutes and then said, "but without him I would be lost— my whole life depends on him and Sara—I've lost out on everything else."

Martha continued to cry. After a few minutes she wiped her eyes and said, "Is this why I hate Sara so much? Is it that I really hate Tom and the marriage, and the person I've become? Maybe I blame the poor kid for the whole mess."

On the next visit Martha was angry. She accused Dr. Rauch of attempting to destroy her marriage. "I was very happy with Tom and with my marriage until I started to see you, and now I don't know how I feel. I'm not going to come back any more if what you are trying to do is destroy our marriage." Then she left.

The next day Martha telephoned Dr. Rauch and hysterically told him that she had beaten Sara very badly. Dr. Rauch encouraged her to return to his office and scheduled an appointment for that evening. Both Tom and Martha appeared. Martha insisted that Tom talk to Dr. Rauch. But Tom was irritated. He didn't think there was anything seriously wrong, that Martha simply had to "settle down and behave decently toward Sara."

Tom was excused and Martha was interviewed privately. She was reasonably composed and apologized for bothering Dr. Rauch earlier that day. "I just lost my head for a little while, but I'll be OK now. I don't need to come back any more." Dr. Rauch attempted to persuade her that she was living in an intolerable situation. He recapitulated the problems Martha had discussed with him, pointing out that further episodes of explosive behavior would occur unless she found ways of making her life more satisfying and meaningful. Martha refused to accept this. She said that she had made up her mind to succeed as a wife and mother and that she was definitely terminating therapy.

Dr. Rauch was afraid Martha would injure Sara seriously and that even if this did not happen, her hatred of the child would produce permanent psychological damage. He believed he should intervene in the matter, but was concerned about his ethical position in doing so. The information that he had received from Martha was a privileged communication; he was dubious of the propriety of reporting his fears to the appropriate authorities. He made several efforts to persuade Martha to continue therapy, but she refused. At last he decided that the safety of the child was of primary importance and warned Martha that he was going to advise the appropriate juvenile authorities of his fears.

Dr. Rauch made contact with the Juvenile Affairs Bureau and told them that he questioned Martha's ability to control her rage and that he was afraid Sara would be seriously injured or even killed.

Mrs. Fredericks, a caseworker, was assigned to investigate. When she arrived at the Nauck home, she found Martha distraught. She had lost her temper again that morning and had brutally whipped Sara. She freely confessed to Mrs. Fredericks that she should not be trusted with the child and agreed that Mrs. Fredericks should take custody of Sara and place her temporarily in the Wilson Shelter for Children.

Tom was outraged when he learned what had been done with Sara. He slapped and beat Martha until she pleaded for him to stop. He phoned both his and Martha's parents and told them what had been done and asked for their help. They arrived at the Nauck home spewing advice and exhortations. It was decided to protest the action of the Juvenile Affairs Bureau, and both sets of parents united in convincing Martha that she had been shiftless and irresponsible in surrendering the child to Mrs. Fredericks.

A preliminary hearing was held on January 6, 1971, with referee James Roller presiding. The state was represented by Deputy District Attorney Raymond Hazel. John Matto was the attorney representing the Nauck family. Tom, Martha, and their daughter Sara were present. The only witnesses were Dr. Rauch, Mrs. Fredericks, and Tom and Martha.

Tom testified that his wife was overly conscientious and that she never really punished Sara with undue severity. Martha said she had been concerned about her feelings, but that she had never really hurt the child. She denied many of the fears and emotions that she had discussed with Dr. Rauch. Mrs. Fredericks testified as to her conversations with Martha and Dr. Rauch. Dr. Rauch voiced his fears, and a ruling was given.

STATE CIRCUIT COURT
Juvenile Division

In the Matter of   )   *No. 79,847*
   Thomas and Martha Nauck) DISPOSITION AND ORDER
   and daughter Sara   )

The above entitled matter having been heard on the *6th* day of *January 1971,* upon the petition of *Juvenile Affairs Bureau* praying that an investigation be made of the circumstances concerning the above named minor, the following persons being present at the hearing: *Thomas, Martha, and Sara Nauck; John Matto, Attorney; Deputy District Attorney Raymond Hazel; witnesses.*

and it appearing to the Court, and the Court finding that:

1. Due notice of this proceeding has been given all persons interested herein.
2. The minor is a citizen of this county and under the jurisdiction of the Court.

The Court being fully advised in the premises:

NOW THEREFORE IT IS HEREBY ADJUDGED AND ORDERED:

Based upon the testimony offered the court finds that Sara Nauck has not suffered unusual or severe punishment. The court also finds Thomas and Martha Nauck competent and concerned parents, and their daughter Sara is ordered returned to their care and supervision.

Dated this *7th* day of *January 1971.*

/S/ *James Roller*
_____
Referee

Following the hearing, Roller had coffee with Matto and Hazel. He was worried about his decision. "I hope nothing happens to that little girl. She was sweet, wasn't she? You know, when people go to a head shrinker, they talk about all sorts of strange things, weird fears and ideas. I didn't see how we could take the daughter from her because of what she said on a psychiatrist's couch."

On January 28 the police were summoned to Holy Angel's Hospital at the request of Dr. Herman Michaels, a resident on emergency service.

DEPARTMENT OF PUBLIC SAFETY
BUREAU OF POLICE
Officer's Report

1. Specific Crime	2. Place of Occurrence	3. Case No.
Assault	2611 Wyatt Ct.	94–9122

4. Date and Time Crime Occurred	5. Date and Time Crime Reported
1/28/71 About 10:00 AM	1/28/71 11:30 AM

6. Victim's Name	7. Person Reporting Crime
Sara Nauck Age 6	Dr. Herman Michaels Holy Angels Hosp.

8. Witnesses' Names	9. Suspect(s) Name
None	Mrs. Martha Nauck 2611 Wyatt Ct.

10. Narrative of Crime, Describe Evidence, Summarize Details Not Given Above.

At 11:30 AM received a 219 put out by Radio Div. Proceed to Holy Angels Hospital and interviewed complainant, Dr. Herman Michaels. Was advised that victim had been brought to hospital with serious head wound. Dr. Michaels stated that mother, Martha Nauck, had admitted striking child with heavy

11. Continuation of Officer's Report
electric frying pan. Was further advised that
Martha Nauck and her husband Thomas were present in
waiting room.

Interviewed Mrs. Nauck and advised her that I was
a police officer investigating injury to her child
Sara. Fully advised her of her rights. She waived
all rights and stated that she had struck child
while angry. Said had hit child with heavy frying
pan. Placed Mrs. Nauck under arrest and advised
husband of procedure for bail. Proceeded with Mrs.
Nauck to her residence and picked up weapon, then
placed Mrs. Nauck in City Jail, charged with
Assault.

Dr. Michaels will advise Dept. if victim dies.

/S/ David Irenton
Badge No. 763
Day relief

2:00 PM 1-28-71

Martha was tried on a charge of aggravated assault. She
waived her right to a jury and pleaded guilty. She was
given a suspended sentence of six months and her daughter
Sara was made a ward of the Juvenile Court. Sara's skull
was fractured and the left temporal lobe of her brain was
damaged. Surgery was necessary, but the actual tissue damage was irreversible. As she recovered she had some impairment of her right leg and right hand. Psychological testing
revealed that she had aphasic symptoms and that there
was impairment of her abilities to perform abstract reasoning and that her memory was impaired.

Sara was released from the hospital after five weeks. She
was placed in the Wilson Shelter for Children and a hearing in the Juvenile Court was scheduled for March 10.

The press had covered Martha's trial, and one newspaper

had expressed editorial outrage. But the press and public did not know that the question of custody for Sara was yet to be decided in the Juvenile Court where the press and public would be excluded.

STATE CIRCUIT COURT
Juvenile Division

In the Matter of	)	*No. 79,916*
Thomas and Martha Nauck	)	DISPOSITION AND ORDER
and daughter Sara	)	

The above entitled matter having been heard on the *10th* day of *March 1971,* upon the petition of *Police Dept.* praying that an investigation be made of the circumstances concerning the above named minor, the following persons being present at the hearing: *Thomas, Martha, and Sara Nauck; John Matto, attorney; Deputy District Attorney Henry Sanderson; witnesses.*

and it appearing to the Court, and the Court finding that:

1. Due notice of this proceeding has been given all persons interested herein.

2. The minor is a citizen of this county and under the jurisdiction of the Court.

The Court being fully advised in the premises:

NOW THEREFORE IT IS HEREBY ADJUDGED AND ORDERED:

1. Martha Nauck did commit an assault upon her daughter, Sara, causing her serious physical harm. Therefore, this child is made a ward of this court and will be returned to her parents' home.

2. Mrs. Nauck is admonished to refrain from using physical punishment.

3. This arrangement will be supervised by the Welfare Dept.

Dated this *11th* day of *March 1971.*

/S/ *Russell Proctor*
_____

Judge

When Sara was returned home, Martha and Tom noticed a great change in her behavior. She was restless and hyperactive, and it was difficult for her to fall asleep at nights. Once she did fall asleep, she was difficult to awaken, and she frequently wet the bed. Her hyperactivity was a continuing irritant to Martha, who, after Sara had been home two weeks, beat her severely.

After her temper subsided, Martha was in despair. She realized that she could no longer control herself and that almost certainly she would inflict additional harm to Sara. She was overwhelmed with feelings of guilt and retreated to her sanctuary—the bathroom. She opened the medicine cabinet and began to take pills, every pill that was in every bottle. The results of this suicide attempt were extreme nausea. She was vomiting uncontrollably when Tom arrived home. He immediately had her hospitalized. As she recovered, her shame and depression were so great that she told Mrs. Fredericks that she had beaten Sara again.

Overwhelmed with concern about Sara, Mrs. Fredericks was determined to make a final effort to rescue her from her precarious situation. The child was picked up and returned to the Wilson Shelter and a petition was prepared for the Court requesting permanent placement in a foster home.

The hearing was held on March 30, with Judge Leo Stern

presiding. Judge Stern was a former criminal lawyer who had spent his days in the hallways of the criminal courts building hustling clients among the petty criminals who were awaiting trial or arraignment. He had been appointed a judge as a result of faithful political service.

At the hearing Tom and Martha were again represented by attorney John Matto. The Deputy District Attorney was Thomas McGovern. Dr. Rauch, Dr. Phillip Green of Holy Angels Hospital, and Mrs. Fredericks were summoned to testify.

Dr. Rauch repeated his fears for Sara's safety and discussed in detail his impressions of Martha's emotional problems. Dr. Green testified as to the injuries Martha had previously inflicted on Sara. Mrs. Fredericks testified as to the statements Martha had made following her suicide attempt. Judge Stern's order was issued on April 1, an appropriate date.

STATE CIRCUIT COURT
Juvenile Division

In the Matter of	)	*No. 80,014*
Thomas and Martha Nauck	)	DISPOSITION AND ORDER
and daughter Sara	)	

The above entitled matter having been heard on the *30th* day of *March 1971,* upon the petition of *Welfare Dept.* praying that an investigation be made of the circumstances concerning the above named minor, the following persons being present at the hearing: *Thomas, Martha and Sara Nauck; John Matto, attorney; Deputy District Attorney Thomas McGovern; witnesses.*

and it appearing to the Court, and the Court finding that:

1. Due notice of this proceeding has been given all persons interested herein.

2. The minor is a citizen of this county and under the jurisdiction of the Court.

The Court being fully advised in the premises:

NOW THEREFORE IT IS HEREBY ADJUDGED
AND ORDERED:

Testimony offered indicates that Mrs. Nauck did punish her daughter Sara by spanking her, but that this occurred at a time of great stress preceding a suicide attempt. This suicide attempt is scarcely a concern of this court.

Dated this *1st* day of *April 1971.*

/S/ *Leo Stern*
——————————————————————
Judge

As a result of this order, Sara is once again in her mother's custody. Martha's hatred for the child is continually exacerbated by Sara's hyperactivity and other behavior resulting from brain damage. Martha resists continuing therapy, and Dr. Rauch and Mrs. Fredericks await reports of further injury to the child.

Chapter 4   OTTO HEINZ

> The girl was not my daughter, you see, she was my step-daughter and when she was about thirteen she really got boy crazy. So my wife figured that as long as I had been fixed and couldn't have children it would be better if I took care of her rather than having some boy getting her knocked up. So every two or three days I would go to bed with her just to keep her satisfied. Sometimes her mother would be there and tell the girl what to do and sometimes she wouldn't. It was different with the seven-year-old girl. I just got crazy putting it in her mouth, and she liked it too, but sometimes I had to give her candy or spank her to get her to do it.
>
> —*Testimony of Otto Heinz*

Elizabeth Adams did not actively dislike her new step-father; she preferred to ignore him. Before Otto Heinz married her mother he seemed rather cool. He occasionally gave her a gift, and one memorable night he had lent her his car. After the marriage his attitude changed. He attempted to assume increasing control over her. He often teased her about her boy friends, asked where she had been whenever she left the house, and was embarrassingly frank in his qustions about her sexual behavior. He had become a drag, someone to be avoided.

On May, 15, 1970 Elizabeth returned home from a school dance at about 1:00 a.m. She kissed her boy friend good night and entered the house. Both her mother and her step-father were waiting for her. At 1:30 neighbors, hearing Elizabeth's screams, called the police.

DEPARTMENT OF PUBLIC SAFETY
BUREAU OF POLICE
Officer's Report

1. Specific Crime	2. Place of Occurrence	3. Case No.
Assault	27913 Washington Ave. N.E.	93-2141

4. Date and Time Crime Occurred	5. Date and Time Crime Reported
5/15/70 between 1:00 and 1:30 AM	5/15/70 1:30 AM

6. Victim's Name	7. Person Reporting Crime
Elizabeth Adams db 2/11/53	Paul Fleser 27917 Washington Ave. N.E.

8. Witnesses' Names	9. Suspect(s) Name
Victim	Otto Heinz (step father of victim) Grace Heinz (mother of victim)

10. Narrative of Crime, Describe Evidence, Summarize Details Not Given Above.

At 1:33 AM, date, received a 219 from Radio Div. Proceed to Washington Ave. address and was admitted to dwelling by Mr. Otto Heinz. Found Elizabeth Adams lying on bed screaming. She was nude except for brassiere. Body covered with welts and bruises, lips cut, nose bleeding. Otto and Grace Heinz stated that she had been attacked by an intruder which they had frightened off. Noted Mr. Heinz had blood on shirt and knuckles of right hand were skinned.

Elizabeth Adams remained incoherent and could not obtain statement. Summoned police ambulance and Elizabeth Adams transported to County Hospital.

Suspect parents committed this crime. Recommend Elizabeth Adams be interrogated as soon as her condition makes possible.

　　　　　　　　　/S/ Harold Mills
　　　　　　　　　Badge No. 554
　　　　　　　　　Car 13 – 2nd nite relief

6:00 AM 5/15/70

By May 16 Elizabeth had recovered sufficiently to make a statement to the police. She stated that upon her return home she was advised by her mother that she was boy crazy and that Otto would take care of her sexual needs in the future. When she protested, Otto ripped off her clothes and began to beat her.

Otto and Grace Heinz were arrested and a routine investigation of their previous records was conducted. This revealed that Grace Heinz had only one previous arrest, for drunken driving.

Otto Heinz had an extensive record. It appeared that he had been a consistently successful suitor, and each of his seven wives was in agreement about the impression that he created prior to their marriage. They described his wistful, boyish charm, his attractive appearance, his normal sexuality, his love for them, and his apparent desire for an enduring, happy marriage.

In each instance the woman Otto sought had been previously married and had children as a result of that marriage, including at least one girl. Otto always expressed interest in these children and the hope that they could learn to love him as if he were their real father. He explained that he could never have children of his own because his first wife had insisted that he have a vasectomy, and he hoped that his potential stepchildren could become substitutes for the natural children he could never father.

After each marriage it turned out that Otto was an alcoholic and an extreme sexual deviate. He followed a consistent pattern in revealing his personality to each of his newly acquired brides. He would become intoxicated immediately after the wedding ceremony and on the wedding night, while drunk, insist that his wife submit to anal intercourse and cooperate in acts of fellatio or cunnilingus. He would refuse to participate in coitus.

If his bride was disappointed or outraged at his behavior, he would become repentent and excuse himself because he was drunk and not fully aware of what he was doing. However, he would continue to drink and continue his attempts to persuade his wife to gratify his sexual demands. If she continued to refuse, he would eventually stop drinking, precipitate a quarrel, and leave.

If his wife submitted to his requests, either gleefully or reluctantly, his sexual appetites became increasingly bizarre. It appeared that he obtained great satisfaction when his wife would crawl to him, open his fly, and commit fellatio while she was on her knees and he was standing erect. After his wife had cooperated in this for awhile, Otto would begin to explain to his wife that an act of love such as theirs was so great that it should be shared or at least witnessed by others. In some instances he attempted to persuade his wife to perform in the presence of friends or to demonstrate her love in the presence of her children.

Otto's sadistic sexual appetite for children became manifest during his fifth marriage. His nine-year-old stepdaughter was left alone with him. When her mother returned, she found that Otto was gone and that the girl had been attacked and badly beaten. Her external genitals had been bitten, and her anus was torn and bleeding as a consequence of an act of rape.

The girl was hospitalized, and the attending physician reported the matter to the police. When the girl was interrogated, she said: "Daddy Otto and I had been playing a word game while Mom was gone. It was a game that he invented—we tried to guess all the different meanings to a word. He would say a word, and I would try to think of all the different things that it could mean. If he could think of something else that I didn't know, then he won. But even if he won, he always let me say the next word, and then he would try to guess all it meant.

"Finally, it was his turn again and he said that the word was love. I tried to guess what it meant, but he said I was all wrong, and he would show me what love was. Then he took my clothes off and took his clothes off. I got scared because I didn't know what he was doing exactly, and I knew Mom wouldn't want me in the front room without any clothes on. So I said I had to stop and do my homework. Then his face got red and he started hitting me, and he grabbed me and bit me. Then he hit me some more and I don't remember what happened until I woke up here at the hospital."

A warrant was issued for Otto's arrest. The police found him at a dance organized by a club for "singles." He was extremely cooperative and courteous when arrested, addressing all of the police officers as "sir" and readily admitting his guilt. In making his confession he stated that he knew that he was insane and that he had been insane for years.

At the preliminary hearing Otto told the judge he had no money for a lawyer and requested that the court appoint one for his defense. This was done, and the court also ordered a psychiatric evaluation.

During the psychiatric interview Otto denied that he was insane. He insisted that he had feigned insanity while talking to the police because he was afraid they would beat him. He maintained that he was one of the few fortunate people in the world who knew the true meaning of love and that real love had to include the exchange of sexual experiences between all members of the family. He believed his stepdaughter had resisted his advances because her true nature had been warped by contact with the crazy world in which she lived and that it was his duty to reeducate her. He excused his brutality by claiming that he was not really angry at her, but that he became enraged at a society that had turned this girl into such an inhibited, loveless deviant, into a creature who would not share his love.

He discussed his penis and his feelings about it straight-forwardly and in detail. He explained that his penis was another manifestation of his true self and that when it stood "proud and erect," he too felt strong and proud and upright. Any act of love and submission to his penis was an act of love and submission to him, and any rejection of his penis by any person of any age or any sex was a rejection of him.

At the trial Otto's attorney entered a plea of not guilty by reason of insanity. The psychiatrist who had examined Otto testified that he was psychotic, that he was incapable of understanding the nature of his acts, and that he con-stituted a continuing danger to others in the community. The horrified judge was easily convinced that Otto's be-havior was that of a madman, acquitted him of the charge and committed him to a state mental hospital.

The hospital to which Otto was sent, like most state mental hospitals in the United States, could be considered a treat-ment facility only by the most generous or imaginative per-son. The patient-professional staff ratio was over 60 to 1. The only trained psychiatrist on the staff was the director, who was ceaselessly engaged in wallowing through a swamp of reports, budgets, complaints, inquiries, and other minutiae. The other physicians on the staff had no formal psychiatric training. Many were immigrants with formidable language difficulties, while others were native-born physicians who had failed in private practice.

Despite their serious limitations, these physicians at-tempted to be of service to their patients, but their lack of skills, coupled with the enormous number of patients as-signed to each doctor, made their efforts a tragic farce ex-cept for the prescribing of tranquilizers or antidepressants. These drugs effectively modify mood and behavior and

make patients more manageable while they are hospitalized, but they do not effect any permanent change in personality. Except for transient neuroses such as depression
and anxiety, medication of this type is no more than a
crutch which enables a person who is crippled mentally or
emotionally to hobble along for a while; when the medication is stopped, psychotic or disordered thoughts and behavior reappear.

Other professional staff members were equally handi-
capped. Work in a state hospital is at the very bottom of
the pecking order among psychologists. The few with
Ph.D.'s who worked at the hospital did so because it was
an excellent source of subjects for research projects or because they were unable to find employment elsewhere.
Others, who had dropped out of school after obtaining a
master's degree, were often quite competent, but lacked
real authority. Like the physicians, they were overwhelmed
by the number of patients assigned to them. The few social
workers who had obtained graduate degrees were usually
assigned to quasi-administrative tasks, which limited their
contact with the patients.

In this situation the most significant persons in contact
with the patients are the ward attendants. Attendants are
poorly paid. The educational requirements for the position
are minimal, usually a high school diploma or an equiva-
lency certificate. Many are quite sympathetic with the patients, are interested in their welfare, and as a result of experience and in-service training, achieve great skill in ward
management. They often offer patients sound, practical advice, and listen attentively to their troubled stories. In
other instances attendants seek these positions to fill their
own emotional needs and derive satisfaction from the authority they have over the patients in their wards. Such attendants are seldom responsive to the needs of the patients

and have little contact with them other than to order them about. Almost always, the behavior of the patient as reported by the attendant is an important factor in treatment and discharge planning.

Otto quickly learned how to become a "good patient." He willingly performed all of the unpaid maintenance jobs that were assigned to him under the euphemistic phrase "work therapy." He avoided discussing sexual matters. He repeatedly assured the attendants that he knew that he had done some "wrong, crazy things," but that it would never happen again. He succeeded in creating the impression that he was an affable, hard-working man who was in firm contact with reality.

At the end of 60 days Otto was interviewed twice by a physician and once by a psychologist. No medication had been prescribed, and he had not been involved in any group or individual psychotherapy. His condition was discussed at a staff meeting and he was judged to be free of any psychosis or neurosis. A diagnostic label of "Personality Disorder, with Sexual Deviations" was applied. It was decided that he had received maximum benefit from hospital treatment, and he was discharged.

No further legal action could be taken against him. His wife divorced him, and he was free. He moved to another city to search for a new job and a new wife. He found both.

Otto's sixth marriage was made in heaven—the sort of heaven that could be envisioned by his tortured mind. Sally was the mother of two daughters, and her sexual behavior was as twisted and deviant as Otto's.

Sally had been sexually molested by her father when she was 12 and subsequently became his willing, enthusiastic bed partner. This incestuous relationship was discovered, and Sally was placed in a foster home. She then shifted her attentions to boys in her own age group on a more or less "come one, come all" basis. She was shifted from one foster home to another as the foster parents became aware of their inability to control her promiscuity.

During this period she was also involved in several homosexual relationships. It was also reported that she had made sexual advances toward younger children of both sexes. Despite this intense experimental sexual activity, Sally never achieved an orgasm. Her sexual experiences tended to produce a high level of tension and arousal instead of satiety and peace. As she matured she became a hyperactive nymphomaniac, constantly seeking, but never finding, sexual satisfaction and release.

Sally became pregnant when she was 16. The father was a naive, 17-year-old boy who was virtually an innocent bystander. He married Sally and endured her demands for a year after the child, Stella, was born. Then he got a divorce, charging infidelity.

Sally found and exhausted two other husbands before she met Otto. A second daughter, Gloria, was born during her third marriage. When she met Otto, Stella was 12 and Gloria was six. Sally married Otto three weeks after meeting him.

During the year and a half they were together, Otto and Sally drank heavily, fought often, abused or ignored Gloria and Stella, and engaged in the wildest variety of sexual behavior. After they had exhausted the possibilities of their own bodies they joined a variety of "clubs" which provided settings in which wife trading, sadism, bisexuality, voyeurism, and exhibitionism were enthusiastically practiced. After a time the children were involved, and both of the girls were required to have sexual relations with Otto, usually in Sally's presence.

One evening, in a relaxed, drunken, confidential mood, Otto related some of his sexual adventures to one of his neighbors. The neighbor was a rigid conformist to socially acceptable sexual mores. When Otto mentioned his sexual experiences with Gloria and Stella, the neighbor became enraged, knocked Otto down, and kicked him in the face; then he called the police.

Otto and Sally attempted to deny to the police that Otto had been sexually molesting the girls, but during the police interrogation Stella said that she had been made to have sexual intercourse with Otto. This enraged Otto who screamed at her, "We didn't make you—you loved it." After this outburst he confessed, as did Sally, and they were arrested and charged—Otto with rape, Sally with contributing to the delinquency of a minor and child abuse.

Once again the court appointed a defense attorney and a psychiatric evaluation was ordered. The psychiatrist found that both Otto and Sally were dangerous sexual deviates, but that they were legally sane in that they were able to understand the nature of their acts and to understand that they had been committing criminal offenses.

While awaiting trial the Heinzes were released on bail and the children were placed in a holding facility. As the date of the trial approached, Sally became severely depressed. She ate very little, became listless and apathetic and increasingly concerned with thoughts of worthlessness and guilt. Late one night, while Otto slept, she climbed into the bathtub, slashed her wrists, and died.

At the trial a plea of guilty was entered. Otto testified in his own defense and stated that he and his late wife were essentially good, respectable people, but they had become alcoholics and the sexual offenses committed against the children occurred at times when both he and Sally were extremely intoxicated. Gloria and Stella offered partial support to this statement, in that they testified that Otto and Sally were drunk nearly all of he time.

The jury was unmoved by Otto's pleas. The judge, taking

into account Otto's previous record, sentenced him to prison for 10 years to life, the sentence to be served in a maximum security hospital for the criminally insane.

The hospital frightened Otto. The walls of the ward were covered with old, flaking green paint, and the tattered, worn furniture was bolted to the floor so that it could not be used as weapons by disturbed patients. Many of the patients were in a state of catatonia or manic excitement and were often shackled to their beds or to chairs. The attendants were big, tough, and ruthless in suppressing any prohibited activity.

Nights were hell. Shackled patients lay in their beds and howled; others paced the floor ceaselessly muttering nonsense. Attendants were on duty, but they sometimes dozed; at these times sudden, savage acts of violence often occurred. Night after night Otto lay in bed, afraid to sleep, dreaming of the past, and devising plans for escape.

Two weeks after his arrival Otto was given a battery of psychological tests and was interviewed by a staff psychiatrist. He was bluntly told that he suffered from an extreme character disorder and that there was no known treatment that would help him. He would be confined for life unless the parole board recommended his release and that could not occur until he had served at least seven years of his sentence. He would be expected to conform to every rule and accept a fulltime work assignment. If he failed to do this, he would be disciplined appropriately.

Otto was assigned to the janitorial force. Every day he joined a group of other patients under the supervision of a guard. They went from ward to ward, cleaning the feces-smeared walls and floors, the filthy bathrooms, always mopping, sweeping, scrubbing. While at work Otto carefully observed security measures, locks, the behavior of the guards, and traffic in and out of the hospital. He could find no loophole, no escape.

The prisoners were allowed a few minor privileges which were contingent on their behavior. A movie was shown each week, selected television programs were available, and a sack of tobacco and cigarette papers were issued daily. As the months passed and Otto became habituated to the hospital, he came to value these privileges and worked hard to obtain them. He was afraid of the guards and attendants and treated them with respectful obedience. He became known as a "good" prisoner, as he had earlier been a "good patient," one who worked hard, kept his mouth shut, and never caused trouble.

Eventually Otto learned from another prisoner that Alcoholics Anonymous held two meetings each week at the hospital. He applied for permission to attend and the permission was readily granted. As is generally known, Alcoholics Anonymous is an influential organization of persons who have had drinking problems and who have banded together to formulate a program that will not only permit them to remain sober, but also to assist other alcoholics to obtain and maintain sobriety. The organization is heavily engaged in proselytizing. Its members visit skid rows, jails, prisons, and hospitals in an effort to assist others with their addictive problems.

The meetings of AA are held in an atmosphere of easy conviviality; all members are addressed only by their first names. An expressed desire to attain sobriety insures acceptance by the group on terms of complete equality. Thus, at a meeting one might find a physician, a priest, a lawyer, a skid row bum, and persons with extensive criminal records associating on terms of complete equality.

The meetings of this organization might be described as a combination of structured group therapy and a public confessional. While the format of the meetings varies from place to place, in general, each member attending describes the self-defeating, destructive life he led during the period he was drinking heavily and then describes the beneficial changes that have occurred since he obtained sobriety. There are certain rules (known as the Twelve Steps) and principles (Twelve Traditions) with which members attempt to comply. Members are encouraged to avoid long-term resolutions and pledges, and instead to attempt to lead a decent, sober life one day at a time.

Many dedicated, humane members of AA who had attained varying degrees of success in life visited the prison where Otto was confined to participate in the AA meeting held there. They frequently brought small gifts, such as "tailor-made" cigarettes, candy, and an abundant supply of coffee. Prisoners attending the meetings passed from the repressive atmosphere of a maximum security prison into a semisocial atmosphere where they were accepted as equals by persons from "outside." The AA members often assured the prisoners that they had no problems except that of alcoholism, and offered a program that would arrest the effects of the alcoholic addiction. They were urged to view alcoholism as a disease, and by logical extension, to see themselves as persons who had been sick, but whose illness could be arrested. The patients were not crazy, not criminals, not twisted, disturbed characters; rather, they were suffering from an insidious disease that infected members of every social strata seemingly at random. Thus the AA argument ran.

The approach of AA had a powerful appeal for Otto. It afforded him an excuse for his behavior while providing contacts with the outside world, with people who treated him as a fellow human being. He attended every meeting, actively recruited members among the patients, and frequently described lurid episodes from his drunken past at the AA meetings.

One of the steps suggested by AA to arrest alcoholism is the Fifth Step, which reads, "Admitted to God, to ourselves, and to another human being the exact nature of our wrongs." Otto selected a prestigeous attorney who was an active member of AA as the other human being to which he would admit the exact nature of his wrongs. He related a highly edited account of his past, placing exaggerated emphasis on the role alcohol had played in shaping his behavior and expressing the greatest repentance for his conduct.

The attorney was a shrewd choice for a confidant. As Otto continued to attend AA, express the acceptable dogma, and recruit additional members, the attorney became convinced that Otto was completely rehabilitated. He determined to secure his release.

The conditions of Otto's sentence precluded the possibility of parole, but the peculiarities of the law did permit probation. Pressure was put on the judge who had pronounced the sentence, and Otto was placed on trial probation until he became eligible for parole. The terms of probation were strict. Otto was prohibited from being present on any premises where alcoholic beverages were sold or consumed. He was forbidden to ever be alone in the company of any female under 21. He was prohibited from attending any movie or other sort of theatrical performance that could be considered lewd or suggestive. He was also forbidden to associate with prostitutes, sexual deviates, or persons who had been convicted of any sort of felony. He was required to report to the probation officer every week and was forbidden to leave the state.

Friends in AA found Otto a menial job as a freight handler with a trucking company. The work was hard, but Otto was equal to it. During slack periods he helped the loading dock foreman with a variety of clerical duties and rapidly learned simple but useful skills incident to the load-

ing and dispatching of trucks. He was promoted to assist-
ant dock foreman after eight months.

During this period he maintained his close ties with AA
and attended several meetings each week. He became something of a prized speaker because his past as an alcoholic
was so lurid and disreputable and his rehabilitation within
AA seemed so complete.

After Otto had worked two years for the trucking company a decision was made to move the trucking operation
to a neighboring state. Otto was one of those invited to
move with the company and to continue his job at the new
location. But the move would be in violation of the terms
of his probation. Otto discussed this with his probation
officer and pointed out that he had made a fresh start, had
stopped drinking, and that he was holding a fairly responsible job. He questioned his ability to find another job in
view of his record and requested permission to make the
move with his employer.

The probation officer had come to view Otto as a "good
risk" and conferred with the probation officials in the
neighboring state where Otto wished to move. It was
agreed that the probation would be transferred to the
neighboring state and that that state would assume supervision of Otto's activities.

Six weeks after Otto moved to his new home he was arrested for drunken driving. His new probation officer rou-
tinely viewed this as a violation of the terms of probation
and had Otto transported back to the institution from
which he had been released. His employer intervened on
his behalf, and his friends in AA hastened to point out to
the judge having jurisdiction that this episode represented
a mere "slip," a common enough occurrence in the history
of many alcoholics seeking rehabilitation. After a month's
incarceration Otto was again released on probation and returned to the state where he had been working. His em-

ployer rehired him, and he became more active in AA, enlightening others as to the dangers of overconfidence and the possibility of "slips."

While attending an AA meeting Otto met Grace Adams who was to become the seventh Mrs. Heinz. Grace had an extensive history of alcoholism and emotional disturbance. She had been married twice, and each marriage had resulted in a psychotic break and subsequent hospitalization. Longterm psychotherapy had been recommended, but Grace had a do-it-yourself bent, and belonged not only to AA but to Recovery, Inc., which is a self-help organization for persons with mental or emotional disturbances.

Grace had two daughters. Maria, who was 21, was married and a mother. Elizabeth was 17, in high school, and lived with her mother. Maria was pregnant before her marriage, and Grace was obsessed with the thought that Elizabeth would follow the same pattern. She tortured herself with images of Elizabeth's sexual behavior, and surreptitiously inspected her underwear for evidence to support her suspicions. She carefully watched for evidence that each period of menstruation occurred on schedule and ceaselessly warned Elizabeth about the dangers of sex.

As Grace and Otto became more friendly, she confided her fears to him. He agreed with Grace and reinforced her fantasies that all "boys" were a menace to Elizabeth's precious virginity. Many of these confidential conversations took place just after Grace and Otto had engaged in sexual intercourse.

After three months Grace and Otto became aware of the inevitability of their love for one another, and they were married. One month later the assault on Elizabeth occurred. Following their arrest and while the investigation of their prior records was being made, the Heinzes were released on bail. They immediately drove to the town where the prison in which Otto had been confined was located and made contact with his old probation officer and with his friends in AA.

Both Grace and Otto insisted that Elizabeth had been assaulted by a burglar and that she had lied about Otto because she resented the discipline he had imposed on her. They claimed that Otto had not violated the terms of his probation, but that a rotten, ungrateful girl was trying to have him returned to prison so that she could be free of his supervision.

The probation officer adopted an aloof attitude and concluded that if the terms of Otto's probation had in fact been violated, he had committed a new criminal offense as well, and he would no doubt be prosecuted by the authorities in the state where the offense had been committed. He told Otto he would take no official action.

Elizabeth Adams had been placed in a foster home by the Juvenile Affairs Bureau after she was released from the hospital. While the district attorney was preparing the Heinz case for trial, he conferred with her to discuss the testimony she would present. She told him that she believed both her mother and Otto were insane, but that she would not testify against them because that would result in her mother being put in jail. She was adamant in her decision, and the district attorney, feeling that he could not successfuly prosecute without her testimony, dropped the charges. The Juvenile Court placed Elizabeth in the custody of her natural father. Grace and Otto did not protest the decision.

The two probation departments began to play a childish, passive-aggressive game, each demanding that the other take action. The probation department in the state in which Otto had been incarcerated demanded repeatedly that the state in which the most recent offense occurred prosecute Otto. The other probation department repeatedly explained that the evidence did warrant prosecution for a new crime, but that Otto's probation should be revoked. When this was not done, the department refused to continue supervision, and Otto was once again free of any watchful restraining influences.

These events received some publicity, and Otto was fired by the trucking company, which no longer considered him a suitable employee. He was unable to find another job. After his unemployment compensation was exhausted, he and Grace requested assistance from the Public Welfare Department. In making application for public assistance, Grace stated that she was diabetic and losing her sight. She described her husband as suffering from ulcers, infected teeth, and a recent stroke. Treatment was provided at County Hospital, where it was found that Grace *was* diabetic and her vision was seriously impaired. In contrast, Otto appeared to be in good health except for minor dental caries.

The Heinzes total assets consisted of their clothing and personal effects, a meager amount of furniture, and a $75 equity in a 1964 Oldsmobile. Their application for assistance was granted, and they quickly settled into a pattern of public dependence, eating cheap food, drinking cheap wine, and living as they saw fit.

Several weeks later a welfare worker making a routine call was startled to find Otto happily playing with a young girl who appeared to be four or five years old. Otto explained that it was his wife's granddaughter whose mother had moved to New York and left the girl in their care. Grace was not home; Otto said she was in town shopping.

Knowing Otto's record, the welfare worker immediately called the police and had the child taken to the Juvenile Affairs Bureau. Grace and Otto angrily demanded that the child be returned. A preliminary hearing was held, and an attorney was appointed to represent Grace and Otto. The Welfare Department was ordered to make a complete investigation and report their recommendations, and an investigation of Otto's current mental status was ordered.

In compliance with the court order, a psychological evaluation of Otto was made by Dr. Douglas, a psychologist on the staff of the County Mental Health Out-Patient Clinic.

COUNTY DEPARTMENT OF PUBLIC HEALTH
MENTAL HEALTH OUT-PATIENT CLINIC
(963) 432-1122   763 Fourth Ave. N.W.

Robert Grednoe, M.D., Director

February 12, 1971

Mr. Regis Stuart
Chief Clerk, Juvenile Division
State Circuit Court

Dear Mr. Stuart:

The court has ordered that a psychological evaluation be made of Mr. Otto Heinz, age 46, 27913 Washington Ave., N.E. In compliance with this order Mr. Heinz was interviewed and tested on February 10, 1971.

During the interview Mr. Heinz was friendly and affable and generally behaved as if he were at a social function. There was no evidence of anxiety, depression, or mental confusion, but the subject was quite defensive in that he attempted to blame others for many of his difficulties.

Mr. Heinz discussed three specific cases in which he conceded that he had been sexually involved with a child. In each case he placed a part of the blame on the mother, on the child, or claimed that he was so drunk that he was unaware of the nature of his conduct.

In discussing the present case he described his wife's granddaughter in glowing terms. "She is a lovely little child, with soft, pink skin, a very pretty face; she's real sweet and pretty." It was my impression that his tone and choice of words were those of a lover rather than a step-grandfather.

A battery of psychological tests was administered. It appears that Mr. Heinz's present level of intellectual functioning is in the bright normal range (IQ 117). However, there are gross deficits in his fund of practical knowledge, and the overall range of scores was similar to those often found in chronic, sociopathic underachievers.

The Minnesota Multiphasic Personality Inventory was administered. The validity scores suggest that the subject was attempting to present a picture of a person who is very scrupulous and who has great self-control and high social and moral standards. The highest of the clinical scores were in response to the items on Scales 4 and 9. The cardinal features usually found in persons obtaining such scores are poor impulse control, self-indulgence, anti-social morals and standards, impulsivity, poor frustration tolerance, poor marital and sexual adjustment, resentment of authority, frequent alcoholism, and frequent criminal activities.

It is my opinion that this man is a dangerous sociopath, and I would urgently recommend that the court give attention to the terms of his probation, his past record, and my findings and refuse to permit his granddaughter to remain in his home.

Very truly yours,

/S/ Samuel Douglas, Ph.D.
Senior Staff Psychologist

The case was assigned to the docket of Judge Doris Huber, a kind, concerned individual. She was especially sympathetic to children who were charged with criminal offenses, and exhausted every means of rehabilitation before sentencing a child to any sort of incarceration. She was obsessed with notions of the sanctity of the family and was extremely reluctant to separate a family no matter how destructive the family's pattern of interaction might be.

The formal hearing was held on March 2, 1971, with Judge Huber presiding. Mr. and Mrs. Heinz were present and were represented by attorney Glenn Snyder. The state was represented by Mr. Raymond Hazel, deputy district attorney. A reporter from a local newspaper asked to be present, but on the motion of the defense attorney, was excluded.

The official records of both probation departments, police reports, and the statement of Dr. Douglas were entered into the record without protest from the defense attorney. Representatives from the Welfare Department testified that it would be impossible for their agency to properly supervise a child living in this home and urged foster home placement. No witnesses were offered for the defense, but Mr. Snyder, the defense attorney, offered an eloquent plea for the need to keep "this troubled family together."

The decision of the court was rendered on March 3, 1971.

STATE CIRCUIT COURT
Juvenile Division

In the Matter of)	No. 76,144
Otto and Grace Heinz, and)	DISPOSITION AND ORDER
Susan West, minor)	
grandchild)	

The above entitled matter having been heard on the *2nd* day of *March 1971*, upon the petition of *Welfare Department* praying that an investigation be made of the circumstances concerning the above named minor, the following persons being present at the hearing: *Otto and Grace Heinz; Glenn Snyder, attorney; Deputy District Attorney Raymond Hazel; Welfare Workers John Camello and Ruth Gardner.*

and it appearing to the Court, and the Court finding that:

1. Due notice of this proceeding has been given all persons interested herein.

2. The minor is a citizen of this county and under the jurisdiction of the Court.

The Court being fully advised in the premises:

NOW THEREFORE IT IS HEREBY ADJUDGED
AND ORDERED:

The testimony offered indicated that several years have passed since Mr. Heinz has been convicted for any sexual offenses against children. He has been providing an adequate home for his grandchild, Susan West. Mrs. Heinz is in ill health and needs the comfort and assistance of her husband.

In the opinion of the court it would be a ruthless act to force either Mr. Heinz or Susan West to leave this home.

It is ordered that Susan West be made a ward of this court and placed in the custody of her grandmother, Grace Heinz. It is further ordered that Mrs. Heinz never leave this child alone with Otto Heinz.

The Welfare Department is instructed to supervise this arrangement, and if it is found that Mr. Heinz is ever alone with Susan West, that Susan be taken into custody and returned to the Juvenile Affairs Bureau.

Dated this *3rd* day of *March 1971.*

                              /S/ Doris Huber
_____
                                      Judge
        _____

Upon receiving the court order, the director of the Welfare Department irately wrote to the court, stating in part, "We refuse to become involved in this case where a child is left in the custody of a known child sexual molester. This monstrous ruling virtually insures a sexual attack on Susan West. Since you refused to follow our recommendations, we will not concern ourselves further and will not attempt to supervise this child."

Susan is now alone with Otto and Grace. Grace is usually drunk, and her degree of blindness is increasing. Otto drinks less now and spends more and more time playing with Susan. He has become quite skilled at inventing games for them to play.

Chapter 5 LOUIS TOMPKINS
Age 24 Months

> Most people, and I guess all of the public, believe that we nurses are really hard boiled. Of course, we do get hardened to pain and suffering. If we didn't, we couldn't do the job. But I never saw anything like this. When they unwrapped the body of that child, I couldn't hold it. I had to go and vomit.
>
> *—A nurse's comment*

Raymond Tompkins was a construction foreman. Everyone who worked with him thought that he was "a helluva good guy." He was friendly and cheerful, always ready to help out one of his men who was in trouble. He was extremely generous, loaned money to everyone who needed it, and would always buy several rounds of drinks for the gang at the bar.

While Tompkins was at work on March 2, 1971, he was advised that his two-year-old son Louis was extremely ill and that he should go home at once. He went home, picked up his wife and son, and drove to Holy Angels Hospital. The boy was dead on arrival. The resident on emergency service inspected the body and called the coroner; the coroner notified the police.

DEPARTMENT OF PUBLIC SAFETY
BUREAU OF POLICE
Officer's Report

1. Specific Crime	2. Place of Occurrence	3. Case No.
CHILD NEGLECT (Death)	HOLY ANGELS HOSPITAL	95-6134

4. Date and Time Crime Occurred	5. Date and Time Crime Reported
Apparently throughout life of victim. DOA Holy Angels Hosp. 2:15 PM	3/2/71 2:30 PM

6. Victim's Name	7. Person Reporting Crime
Louis Tompkins (age – 24 months)	Coroner Patrick McKee, M.D.

8. Witnesses' Names	9. Suspect(s) Name
William Hurd, M.D., Holy Angel's Staff Dorothy Pendergrast, R.N., Holy Angel's Staff	Raymond Tompkins (father) Mary Tompkins (mother)

10. Narrative of Crime, Describe Evidence, Summarize Details Not Given Above.
HOME ADDRESS: 2917 Grace Ln.
SIBLINGS OF VICTIM: Jane Tompkins, age 13
Phillip Tompkins, age 12   Greta Tompkins, age 5
MATERNAL UNCLE & AUNT: Robert and Lucille Hopper
6743 E. 49th St.   298-6292

Telephone request from Coroner Patrick McKee
to cover at Holy Angels Hospital emergency room.
Coroner stated he had been called regarding aside
child, Louis Tompkins, who arrived at 2:15 PM, DOA.
Sgt. Arena assigned call to writer. Arrived at Holy
Angels Hosp. at about 3:10 PM. We were directed to
the table where the child was lying by the
supervisor of the emergency room. The cover was
pulled back from the child. We observed a dead,
white, male child that appeared to be the size of a
child six months old. We learned that its actual age
was 24 months.

Victim's rib cage was distended and skin pulled

11. Continuation of Officer's Report

taut all over child's trunk & limbs. Face was hollow
and resembled a skull with eyes and cheeks sunken.
Looked as if it had not eaten for sometime and had
starved to death. The buttocks, privates and legs
were covered with bloody scabs. This child had the
appearance of complete neglect. Three color slides
were taken in the presence of Drs. McKee and Hurd.

Hospital staff reported that there were three
other children in the home. I phoned this
information to Sgt Arena and was told that an
investigation would be made.

The victim's parents, Raymond and Mary Tompkins
were present at Holy Angels Hosp. Advised them that
writer was a police officer making an investigation
of the death of their son and that criminal charges
might be brought against them. They were also
advised that writer would like to question them,
but that they could remain silent if they wished.
They were also advised that they could have an
attorney present if they so desired. They both said
that they understood and that they would talk to me.

Parents stated that the child had not been seen
by a doctor since it was two months old and that was
at the hospital where it was born. They said that
the doctor there had told them that the child was
all right. They admitted that they noticed that the
child was not developing properly at the time that
it was one year old, but they did not take it to a
doctor. They could not give a satisfactory answer
as to why the child did not receive medical attention
except to say that Mr. Tompkins worked for so many
different contractors that it was hard to know if
they had Blue Cross coverage. They did admit taking
another child to a doctor about this past Father's
Day, and they also admitted that Mrs. Tompkins had
been treated at County Hospital several times in the

11. Continuation of Officer's Report

past year. They were asked several times why they
had not asked for medical help for their child, but
gave no answer. They just looked at each other.

At this time Mr. Tompkins said that there were
some very important things at his job that he had to
take care of, and asked if he could leave. He said
that he would be back in one hour. He was told that
he was not under arrest at this time, but he was
asked to return as soon as possible. He was warned
that if he did not return, a warrant might be issued.
After Mr. Tompkins had left Mrs. Tompkins said that
she was very glad to talk to me alone. I let her talk
freely in her own words and at her own pace and
recorded her comments.

"Ray makes $225.00 each week in take home pay, but
he only gives me $15.00 to feed the family and buy
clothes for the kids and me. I never have enough.
He gives me my money Friday night, and we are
always out of food by Monday. I always make sure to
have flour and syrup in the house, so we can eat pan
cakes.

"He don't care if we have enough to eat ; he never
comes home until two in the morning. He always stops
at the 'Four Aces' Tavern after work, and eats
sandwiches there and drinks beer. He always has
enough.

"I don't have a car, and I don't have money for a
baby sitter, so I never get out of the house. Most of
the time one or other of the oldest kids can't go to
school because they don't have clothes. I don't
have money for soap or anything to clean with, so we
just sit around and watch TV, but it's broke now.

"I knew something bad was wrong with little Louis.
I had to wean him when he was real little because
my milk went dry, and he never seemed to want to eat
what the rest of us had. I forced some pan cakes
down a time or two, but he just threw up. He didn't

11. Continuation of Officer's Report

act right. He didn't crawl or talk or nothing, but once in a while he would sit up. I couldn't potty train him, and I didn't have clean diapers to keep changing him. Guess that's how he come to have those sores.

"He used to cry a lot, but seems like the past several weeks he just give up. He just laid there. I knew he needed a doctor bad, and I tried to get one. We don't have no phone, and one day I went to the neighbors and called lots of doctors who were in the phone book, but they all said I would have to bring him in. They didn't make visits at your home. This neighbor told me about three clinics, and I tried them, but they all said I would have to bring the baby in. I couldn't take him anywhere. I didn't have a car and never had no bus fare.

"This morning I knew he was real bad. He tried to lift his head once or twice, but it just sort of fell back. I went to the neighbors and called two more doctors, but they wouldn't come. Then I called this hospital, and they said I better bring the baby in right away. I called Ray at work and told him I thought Louis was dying, and he came home, and we brought him here. They told me he was dead when we arrived, but I didn't know it. He had been so still most of the time anyway.

"Ray never picked the baby up; he never even looked at him. When I tried to get him to take the baby to a doctor, he just said that was my responsibility. He wasn't going to miss work to take the kids anywhere."

Writer asked Mrs. Tompkins if she had ever phoned the police for assistance. She said that she hadn't thought of it. Asked her if she had anything else to say, and she said she didn't. Advised her that we would probably be talking to her further after we received the coroner's report.

11. Continuation of Officer's Report

At this time Mr. Tompkins returned, and he was interviewed privately. The writer warned him once again of his rights, and he said he didn't mind talking to me and that he didn't want an attorney. His statements were recorded.

"Hell, what do I need with a lawyer. All this is my wife's business. I work every day, and she takes care of the house and the children. Sure I'll talk to you.

"All I know is that once in a while my wife said that the baby seemed to be sick, and I told her to take him to a doctor. I didn't know she wasn't feeding him, if that's what it was. She could have told me if she thought he was real sick. I came right away today, didn't I?

"I do a lot for that woman. I don't love her, never did. I married her because she was pregnant, and she begged me to. I stick with her, but I sure as hell would rather get rid of her and be out on my own. I give her her money every week, and if she needs more, she could get a job and work like I do."

Writer asked Mr. Tompkins if he had anything to add, and he said he did not. He was advised that we would talk to him further at another time.

Writer noted that neither of these parents cried at any time and seemed to accept the death of the baby as just a minor irritation. They did not seem to have any feelings or any sense of shame.

Coroner McKee will be sending us a report from his office, and his office will also be taking pictures. THE ONLY PICTURES WE HAVE ARE THE ONES ATTACHED TO THIS REPORT. DO NOT SEPARATE.

/S/ Judith Rosen
Badge No. 6179
Day Relief

6:00 PM   3-2-71

DEPARTMENT OF PUBLIC SAFETY
BUREAU OF POLICE

Officer's Report

1. Specific Crime	2. Place of Occurrence	3. Case No.
Child Neglect	2917 Grace Ln.	95-6134

4. Date and Time Crime Occurred	5. Date and Time Crime Reported
Louis Tompkins DOA Holy Angels this date Ongoing neglect of victim and siblings	3/2/71 3:35 PM

6. Victim's Name	7. Person Reporting Crime
Louis Tompkins, Jane Tompkins, age 13; Phillip Tompkins, age 12; Greta Tompkins, age 5	Officer Judith Rosen

8. Witnesses' Names	9. Suspect(s) Name
Writer, Robert & Lucille Hopper (relatives), and William Roberts, School Principal	Raymond Tompkins (father) Mary Tompkins (mother)

10. Narrative of Crime, Describe Evidence, Summarize Details Not Given Above.

Received call from Officer Rosen who was covering DOA at Holy Angels Hospital advising that there were three more children in home where alleged neglect occurred. Proceeded to 2917 Grace Ln. and interviewed children and observed home.

Found house strewn with garbage and dirty clothing. Investigated kitchen and found no food in house except one half empty sack of flour, a stick of margarine, and a bottle of corn syrup. Only two

11. Continuation of Officer's Report

twin beds in house, sheets dirty, beds not made.
Children said all four of them sleep in one twin
bed, parents sleep in other. Greta Tompkins was
nude when I arrived, but sister, Jane, found old
terry cloth robe for her to wear. None of the
children had shoes that could be worn, and only a
few tattered articles of clothing.

All of the children were frightened and did not
wish to talk to writer. All admitted that they were
hungry, and also that they were cold. There did not
appear to be any heat in the house except the kitchen
oven.

Obvious case of severe neglect. Took children in
my car to the Wilson Shelter for Children.

Went to 6743 E. 49th St. to interview only known
relative, Mr. and Mrs. Robert Hopper. Mrs. Hopper
is aunt of Mrs. Tompkins. Mrs. Hopper not surprised
to find that Louis Tompkins was dead. Said that she
had asked Mary Tompkins to take child to doctor many
times. Said Mr. Tompkins was "real mean" and would
not give Mrs. Tompkins proper amounts of money to
run house properly. Mrs. Hopper said she used to
visit Tompkins home regularly, and when she was
there she would try to clean house and see that
children got something to eat. Said finally got
disgusted and quit visiting.

Proceeded to Woodburn-Kennedy to interview
principal and children's teachers. Learned none of
children attend school regularly and that they
often beg teachers or other pupils for food. Mr.
William Roberts, principal, said had made home
visit and found all children alone and nude. Was
told mother had taken their only clothes to
laundermat. Waited two hours for mother's return.
Said mother advised him it was impossible to have
children in school many days because of lack of
clothing. Mr. Roberts also said he had considered

reporting matter but was afraid to get involved.
Worried that parents would complain to school
board.
   See officer Rosen's report.

                 /S/ Sgt. Joseph Arena
                     Badge No. 1283
                     Day Relief

6:30 PM   3-2-71

The lengthy coroner's report stated, in effect, that Louis Tompkins suffered from diaper rash, herpes simplex, and that death was caused by severe malnutrition. The Wilson Shelter for Children arranged to have a complete medical and psychological evaluation made of the surviving children: Jane, aged 13; Phillip, 12; and Greta, 5.

It was found that Jane's physical development was retarded, that she was suffering from severe malnutrition, and that she was an extremely anxious, frightened child.

Phillip was also retarded in his physical development and also suffered from severe malnutrition. It was further found that he was extremely impulsive, distractible, and had a poor attention span. He talked and behaved in a strange and bizarre manner; it was thought he might be psychotic. During his first week at the Wilson Shelter he had an epileptic seizure. A neurological evaluation was made and it was found that the EEG was abnormal, with wave forms typical of an epileptic disorder. Medication was prescribed.

Greta, like her siblings, also suffered from malnutrition and retarded physical development. Her front teeth were broken off at the gum lines. Her sister Jane said this had occurred when their father hit Greta in the mouth with a padlock. Greta was extremely withdrawn, and it was difficult to induce her to talk to anyone. If she were permitted to do so, she obviously would prefer to spend most of her time curled up on her bed.

The circumstances of Louis Tompkins' death were referred to the grand jury, and Mr. and Mrs. Tompkins were indicted for manslaughter. They appeared for trial on May 27, 1971. The judge declared the indictment to be defective, in that it did not specifically state the time that the alleged offense occurred, and both parents were released. No action was taken by the district attorney to obtain a second indictment, but a petition was prepared to make the children wards of the court. The petition was heard on June 7, 1971.

STATE CIRCUIT COURT
Juvenile Division

In the Matter of	)	*No. 84,114*
Jane, Phillip, and Greta	)	DISPOSITION AND ORDER
Tompkins	)	

The above entitled matter having been heard on the *7th* day of *June 1971,* upon the petition of *Police Dept.* praying that an investigation be made of the circumstances concerning the above named minor, the following persons being present at the hearing: *Raymond and Mary Tompkins (parents); Jane, Phillip and Greta Tompkins (children); Deputy District Attorney Raymond Hazel; Police Officers Judith Rosen and Joseph Arena.*

and it appearing to the Court, and the Court finding that:
1. Due notice of this proceeding has been given all persons interested herein.
2. The minor is a citizen of this county and under the jurisdiction of the Court.
The Court being fully advised in the premises:

NOW THEREFORE IT IS HEREBY ADJUDGED
AND ORDERED:

Evidence presented indicates that—
    1. Louis Tompkins, a two year old child, died of severe malnutrition on March 2, 1971, and that he had been in the care and custody of Raymond and Mary Tompkins.
    2. The Tompkins house is strewn with garbage and the sanitary conditions are below minimal standards.
    3. Jane, Phillip, and Greta Tompkins are suffering from malnutrition and neglect.
Jane, Phillip, and Greta Tompkins are made wards of this court and the responsibility for their care is given to the Welfare Department.

Dated this *7th* day of *June 1971.*

                    /S/ Doris Huber
_____
                                    Judge

Following the action of the court the children were placed in foster homes where, for the first time in their lives, they received adequate medical attention. A special diet was prepared for Jane. Her foster parents, being familiar with the case, almost overwhelmed her with love and affection. Her response was gratifying. She gained weight; she was pathetically proud of her new clothes; and she developed very close ties with her foster parents.

Greta was placed in another foster home. She received extensive dental care, and she too flowered and became a happy little girl.

Phillip Tompkins, however, had difficulty in adjusting to his foster home. He developed nocturnal enuresis (bed-wetting), which was accompanied by frightening nightmares. His behavior became increasingly intolerable. He either withdrew and failed to respond to questions or comments directed to him or became angry and frequently punched, bit, or scratched his foster parents.

He was taken to the County Mental Health Out-Patient Clinic for further evaluation. The clinic concurred with the previous diagnosis that Phillip was suffering from organic brain damage, but it was also believed that he was suffering from a very serious thought disorder, possibly Schizophrenia, Paranoid Type. He was referred to the psychiatric department of the medical school for further evaluation.

While Phillip was in the waiting room of the psychiatric department of the medical school, he suffered an extreme emotional disturbance during which he appeared to believe that he was being placed in jail and that once he was in jail he would be returned to his parents. He attempted to escape and strongly resisted the attendants' efforts to control him. It was necessary to call the police. Because of his disturbed emotional condition, he was taken to a state mental hospital.

The admitting physician at the state hospital agreed that Phillip was quite possibly insane, but pointed out that the open door policy of the hospital, with no locked wards or restraints, precluded admitting such a disturbed person. He recommended that Phillip be taken to the psychiatric wing of the County Hospital.

When Phillip was taken to the County Hospital, the admitting physician said they had no facilities for the care of children; they concerned themselves only with adult psychiatric patients. He refused to admit the boy.

In the absence of any other facility, Phillip was taken to the place of detention operated by the Juvenile Affairs Bureau and confined there for two months. During this period of confinement he was seen weekly by a psychiatrist and appropriate medication was prescribed. This medication failed to control his assaultive behavior, however, and it was felt necessary to keep him continuously confined in his room. This confinement had the effect of making Phillip more suspicious, more angry, and more divorced from reality.

The juvenile authorities petitioned the court for assistance with Phillip. Since there was no suitable psychiatric facility in which the boy could be placed, the judge ordered him confined in the Boys' Industrial School, where he presently is. The school is little more than a jail for children. The attendants and guards are disturbed by Phillip and keep him locked in a cell much of the time. He is seen twice a month by a psychiatrist, who protests vainly over Phillip's continuing enforced isolation. The facility is chronically understaffed, and there are not sufficient guards or attendants available to stay with Phillip if he were to be released from his cell. The only treatment plan is nebulous. It appears that he is to be kept in solitary confinement until he becomes old enough for admission to an adult maximum security psychiatric unit.

Mr. and Mrs. Tompkins are free, and they have another child, a boy named Michael. They are raising this child without any supervision of any sort. Phillip's condition is largely attributable to criminal neglect by his parents, but he remains imprisoned while his parents are free. Little Louis is dead and forgotten.

Chapter 6 JACK SWEENY

Psychological Consultant—Let's cut out the bullshit. This boy
has been arrested sixteen times; everything in the record
indicates that the whole family is screwed up; the case has
been referred to two other consultants who have recommended taking the boy out of the home, and you have done
nothing. Why?

Juvenile Court Counselor—I'm quitting here next week, so I'll
be honest. Mr. Sweeny said he'd kill me if I did anything to
put his son away or break up his family. He's a terrible man,
and I believed him, so I just kept the case sort of buried.

—Excerpt from an interview

Walter Pittock, Ph.D., was a consultant to the Juvenile
Court. He visited the court every week and was usually
assigned three of the agency's more difficult cases for
evaluation. The regular procedure was for him to talk to a
child, to the child's parents, and to review the social history. He would then make suggestions and recommendations to the juvenile court counselors.

On May 12, 1969 Dr. Pittock was assigned the case of
Jack Sweeny, a 12-year-old boy. He was astonished to discover that the boy had been arrested 16 times. In making
the referral to Dr. Pittock, the court counselor, James
Elledge, wrote:

Reason for Referral: The purpose of this request for a psychological evaluation is to determine the direction of future
planning for Jack. He has been arrested 16 times for major
crimes.
General Problem: A dysfunctional family. The parents have
little awareness of their own or the children's problems. The
children, especially Jack, have little concern for rules or regulations. Keith, age 11, and Dennis, age 10, along with Jack,
were first referred to the Juvenile Court in June, 1965, and
have since been referred many times for burglary, larceny,

bike thefts, auto thefts, breaking and entering, and stealing purses from bowling alleys. They boys were in detention this last time from September 13 until October 22, at which time they were returned home. We have attempted to handle this situation with warnings, informal probations, and with attempts to educate the parents in more adaptive ways of controlling their boys' behavior.

Family Background: Mr. and Mrs. Sweeny are from Massachusetts, and this is a first marriage for both. Mr. Sweeney had been a successful mechanical engineer, but he had a serious automobile accident and suffered severe brain damage which resulted in drastic changes in his behavior and personality. He is very easily enraged, and he finds it difficult to remember what he has said or what he has been doing, and as a result, it is very difficult for him to hold a job. He now operates a small shop in which he repairs various types of construction equipment. It is difficult for him to estimate his costs, and as a result, when the job is finished, it is often discovered that he has made little or no profit. In other instances he wildly overestimates the price to be charged and drives potential customers away. He has had to declare bankruptcy three times in the past six years.

Mr. Sweeny's attitude toward his sons is contradictory. When they displease him, he reacts very violently and subjects the children to harsh, outrageous punishment. For example, it is known that on at least two occasions the boys were chained in the garage for over two days. On other occasions he "sentences" his sons to do without food for fairly extended periods of time. He frequently whips them with a belt or strikes them with his fists.

When others, such as the police or counselors of this agency, complain to Mr. Sweeney about the boys' behavior, he becomes extremely defensive and denies that the boys present any problem or that they misbehave in any way. On one occasion two police officers arrived at the Sweeny home to pick up Dennis, who was known to have stolen and sold a bicycle. Mr. Sweeney refused to let the police have Dennis, and an altercation ensued. It was finally necessary for the two police officers to call for assistance, and eventually six officers held Mr. Sweeney down while they took his son from the home. In discussing this affair Mr. Sweeney feels shamed and discusses the humiliation of being subdued by the police with his wife as a witness. Apparently he feels that he should have been able to overcome the six officers and that his failure to do so has resulted in a loss of his wife's esteem. It is our opinion that Mr. Sweeny would like to be a good father and to raise his sons properly, but that his thinking is so deranged that it is impossible for him to do so.

Mr. Sweeny acts in a very hostile, aggressive manner toward women, and on one occasion assaulted one of our women counselors. As a result, only male counselors have been assigned to work with this case.

Mrs. Fern Sweeny, the mother, is a dependent type person, fat and unkempt, who oozes inadequacy. She is not employed and spends her time attempting to keep house, control her sons, and placate her husband. Counselors who have visited the home have reported finding her standing in the middle of the living room flailing about her with a belt as she attempted to control the boys who were darting back and forth teasing her. She, too, can become unusually angry, but she seldom is assaultive. It is believed that her mentality is low, and apparently she was able to function adequately prior to Mr. Sweeny's accident when he was a strong, resourceful husband. Since the accident, the additional problems brought about by Mr. Sweeny's erratic behavior have proven overwhelming to her, and she is presently completely incapable as a wife and mother.

Jack, the boy: Jack is a ward of this court. He is a likable youngster of average size. He has been reported as being hyperactive, but he has no difficulty in controlling his behavior when he is in detention. It is reported that he is socially and academically maladjusted at school. He has been retained in the second grade and again in the fourth grade. He has difficulty in reading, has a short attention span, and psychological testing indicates that he is of low-normal intelligence.

In discussing his home, he frequently expresses great concern for his brothers' well-being. He does not complain about his father, and apparently senses that Mr. Sweeny has many special problems. He is able to discuss some of the punishment meted out by his father without emotion, and frequently states that one of the reasons for his stealing is to get money to feed himself and his younger brothers. Apparently this is at least partially true. On one occasion the four boys were picked up when they attempted to order a meal in a large, fashionable hotel dining room. In addition to their age, they attracted the attention of the hotel personnel because of their unkempt appearance and tattered clothing.

Generally, while in detention Jack is well behaved and follows the rules and regulations with ease. However, he fre-

quently states that he is homesick, and apparently this home-
sickness is partially a result of his anxiety concerning his
younger brothers.
   Conclusion: It is my opinion that we need to take some
direct action to intervene in the family at this time for the
welfare of all four children. I'm not sure whether or not we
can work with the family unit as it remains at the present
time, but I do suspect that in any case the father would
benefit from some type of psychological or psychiatric help.
Resistance from the family and especially from the father is
anticipated, and thus, I would welcome your evaluation and
consultation at this time.

After reading Mr. Elledge's report Dr. Pittock leafed
through the voluminous file and was disgruntled to discover that this case had been referred to other consultants,
but that no action had been taken on their recommendations. It was noted that David Haas, M.D., a child psychiatrist, had considered this case on a previous occasion.

LAKEVIEW CHILD GUIDANCE CLINIC
1320 N. Alistaire Road
(963) 528-9934

October 6, 1967

Mr. Ralph Gilliam
Juvenile Court Counselor
Children's Place of Detention

Dear Mr. Gilliam:
   Jack Sweeny, age 10, was seen at this clinic on October 4,
1967, at your request. It is my understanding that this boy
has been arrested on numerous occasions and has been frequently held at the Children's Place of Detention.
   PAST HISTORY: The past history was obtained from Mrs.
Sweeny who is an extremely obese, untidy woman, who gave
a long history of her problems and multiple reasons why her
boys were always in trouble. Apparently she believes that
everyone with whom her family is involved are either deranged people or persons who are "just plain mean." She is
extremely uninsightful and either lies or is unaware of the

full nature of her children's delinquent behavior and appears completely unaware of how troublesome they may be to others.

Her intelligence is estimated to be in the dull-normal range. Her conversation was extremely disorganized and did not follow any logical direction as she moved from one topic to another. In general, she apparently believes that none of her children are at fault, but that they are continually being victimized by others.

According to Mrs. Sweeny, Jack's birth was normal following a nine month gestation period. Presentation was cephalic with no difficulties. He reached his developmental milestones at appropriate age levels. It was suspected that he had appendicitis approximately one year ago, but otherwise his health has been excellent. He has never been seriously injured nor has he had convulsions. He has no physical deformities.

At the conclusion of the interview, she stated that she did believe that there may have been a mistake in buying the boys bicycles. She believes that since the boys have had the bikes, it has been especially difficult for her to control them because they can get farther away from her and stay away longer.

PSYCHIATRIC INTERVIEW: Jack is a small, well proportioned 10-year-old boy who has a good concept of reality and who showed very little anxiety during the interview. He was unmotivated, extremely distractible, and spent most of his time looking out the window watching traffic. When I could catch his attention, he was cooperative and pleasant. He showed no motility disorder either in large or small muscles. His special senses were grossly intact; his speech was normal, but his language showed poor comprehension and poor acculturation. He read at mid-second grade level which would place him approximately three years behind his expected level of reading. His spelling was at first or early second grade level. His conceptual thinking was poor, but was commensurate with his IQ and motivation. Lateral dominance was fully established, and he was right eyed, right handed, and right legged.

He appeared only superficially interested in the interview. However, he did discuss some of his hopes and aspirations, and it appeared that he had a very sparse fantasy life and a very delinquent orientation. He freely stated that he did not care for his parents, but appeared to be quite affectionate and defensive of his younger brothers. He sees no problem with himself, but projects all of his problems and difficulties onto others, including his father. He stated that the father frequently keeps them without food and as a result they must steal to live.

RECOMMENDATIONS: The long court social history of this family, together with Jack's behavior when he was interviewed, would combine to suggest that this lad may soon develop a very strong sociopathic personality. It is quite obvious that the parents are unable to provide a fit home for these boys, and I would strongly recommend that these boys be made wards of the court and placed in foster homes. In view of Jack's obvious attachment for his younger brothers, I would recommend that if it is at all possible, all of these boys be placed in one home.

Do not hesitate to call on me if I can be of any further assistance.

Very truly yours,

/S/ David Haas, M.D.

As Dr. Pittock continued to study the file, it was apparent that no action had been taken on Dr. Haas's recommendations. His report had been placed in the file and forgotten. Soon after the report was made, Jack and Dennis Sweeny had been arrested once again for stealing purses from a bowling alley. Despite the recentness of Dr. Haas's report, they were held in the Children's Place of Detention, then returned to their home under "house arrest." This meant that they could not leave their home except in the company of an adult, and their parents were admonished to report immediately any infraction of this rule. This house arrest was to continue for a month. Several weeks later all four of the boys were involved in the theft of an automobile. Jack, who was the driver, maintained it was not his fault, that it was the fault of the owner who had left the keys in the car. Apparently it was Jack's argument that if you find a car with keys, there is nothing to do except drive off with it.

Following this incident the boys were again placed under house arrest and the parents were admonished to exert greater control over them. This kept the boys under control for one week; then they stole a school bus.

Jack discovered that after the children living in rural areas had been delivered to their homes, the buses were returned to a parking lot at the rear of the school building and that the keys sometimes were left in the ignition switch. It seemed that a school bus would be a fine thing to have. The seats could be taken out, beds installed, and it would be possible to tour the country in comfort and ease. Unfortunately, after Jack had stolen the bus each of his brothers wanted to drive it. They were too small to see sitting down, and had to drive standing up. This arrangement made it impossible to brake efficiently, and the bus was soon overturned and wrecked. The school officials and the police were seriously alarmed, and the Juvenile Court called another consultant, Dr. Douglas, a psychologist.

COUNTY DEPARTMENT OF PUBLIC HEALTH
MENTAL HEALTH OUT-PATIENT CLINIC
(963) 432-1122   763 Fourth Ave. N.W.

ROBERT GREDNOE, M.D., DIRECTOR

November 16, 1967

Mr. Adam Harrison
Juvenile Court Counselor
Children's Place of Detention

Dear Mr. Harrison:

Jack Sweeny, the 10-year-old son of Patrick and Fern Sweeny, was interviewed and tested by me on November 15, 1967. Jack had been referred for evaluation as a result of a long history of maladaptive and anti-social behavior, the details of which are to be found in his voluminous case record.

Fern Sweeny, Jack's mother, was interviewed by me at your agency on November 14, 1967. It was my impression

that Mrs. Sweeny was an inadequate, uninsightful, poorly informed woman of dull-normal intelligence who is completely
inadequate both as a woman and as a mother. It is impossible to conceive of her as being capable of providing the
necessary home environment for Jack or for her other children. Patrick Sweeney, the boy's father, did not appear for
an interview, and as a result I have not made a personal
evaluation of him. However, the reports in your case history
indicate that Mr. Sweeny is a violent, aggressive, irrascible
individual who has probably suffered extensive brain damage,
and your records strongly suggest that he, too, is completely
incapable of becoming an adequate parent.

Jack is a small, sturdy boy who was quite aloof when I interviewed him. He readily responded to any questions that I
asked, but he did not spontaneously offer any information.
He spoke of his brothers in very kindly, loving terms, but he
was quite defensive regarding his parents. He did state that
his father had a very bad temper, and he admitted that he
and his brothers were often deprived of food in punishment
for their misdemeanors. He really saw no problem with himself and had ready explanations for all of his difficulties. He
apparently truly believes that he is not a "bad boy," but
rather an average, normal kid who just happens to get
caught.

In making a psychological evaluation of Jack a complete
battery of psychological tests was employed. Jack appeared
to make a reasonable effort to answer the questions and perform the tasks required in completing this test battery, and
it would be my opinion that the results are a valid estimate
of his present level of functioning.

The scores obtained by Jack indicated that his present level
of intellectual functioning is in the dull-normal range, with a
Full Scale IQ of 85, a Performance IQ of 93, and a Verbal
IQ of 81. This is at about the 11th percentile of his age group.
The results of the test of visual retention and the visual
motor test indicate that Jack does not have any impairment
of visual memory or visual motor coordination that could be
attributed to organic injury or disease.

The results of the personality tests administered to Jack
and the impressions gained during the interview combined
to suggest that he is a disturbed lad who is in a near psychotic state. He has a very low tolerance for frustrations. He
suffers from intense anxieties, and becomes disorganized
under the slightest pressure. When this occurs, and he does
become disorganized, he regresses to a rather primitive level

and even engages in unrelated physical activity, displays aggressive behavior, or adopts an "I don't care" attitude. He is extremely narcissistic, egocentric, sociopathic, and has strong oppositional tendencies. He exhibited extreme impulsivity, unevenness of development, rapid mood swings, poor judgment, and the lack of ability to develop any really meaningful personal relationships. At this time he does not have any delusions or hallucinations, but his tolerance of frustration is so low that he tends to withdraw to a fantasy world at the slightest provocation. It is very difficult for him to admit that he is in any way responsible for his own behavior or for his own difficulties, and he prefers to place the full blame on others or to deny that his behavior has been objectionable.

It would appear that a major subconscious conflict that Jack cannot resolve is that he hates his father, but he has repeatedly been told that this is wrong, that he should love his father, and that his father is always right. Hence, Jack has been compelled to deny the reality of his own feelings and experiences. He has never learned that he can be an object of love and affection, and he has never learned that there is any possibility of consistency of behavior on the part of adults. Therefore, he sees himself as living in a strange, hostile, unpredictable world in which there is little relationship between an act and its consequences. His intellectual capacity is low, and he is unable to cope with many of the problems that he encounters.

It is my opinion that the home environment provided for this boy is completely unsuitable and that if he is to be salvaged, he must be removed from this home and placed in a controlled, structured environment. If this is not done, it is likely that his tendency toward sociopathic behavior will increase. It is most probable that his brothers are also experiencing the ill effects of the malignant environment of the Sweeny home.

Jack is in an especially precarious emotional state, and if he is placed in a different environment, attempts should be made to involve him in a counseling situation.

To repeat, under no circumstances should these boys be permitted to remain in their malignant home environment.

Very truly yours,

/S/ Samuel Douglas, Ph.D.
Psychological Consultant

After reading Dr. Douglas's recommendations Dr. Pittock refused to proceed with an evaluation of Jack. He argued that previous evaluations had been made by competent people, that no action had been taken, so further evaluation would be a waste of time. Mr. Elledge was newly assigned to the case and could not offer any explanation as to why the recommendations of Drs. Haas and Douglas had not been followed. Dr. Pittock got in touch with Juvenile Court counselor Gilliam who had been in charge of the case in 1967 when the second evaluation was made. Gilliam was reluctant to discuss the case but under some pressure finally admitted that he did not petition the court to remove the children from their parents' home because he feared that Mr. Sweeny would kill him. His fear of Mr. Sweeny caused him to continually attempt to cover up the children's misbehavior and repeatedly to send them home with a warning, no matter how serious the law violations. He also admitted that Mr. Sweeny bragged to him that he had told the children they did not need to worry about the Juvenile Court, that he, their father, had "everything under control."

At Dr. Pittock's insistence a petition was filed with the court asking for wardship of all of the Sweeny children and recommending that they be removed from their parents' home.

A hearing was held on May 22, 1969, with Judge Richard Havens presiding. The deputy district attorney was Mr. Michael Hitchman. The Sweenys were represented by Roy Elkins. Dr. Haas, Dr. Douglas and several Juvenile Court counselors who had been involved in the case testified in support of the petition. Several friends and relatives of Mr. and Mrs. Sweeny testified in their behalf.

STATE CIRCUIT COURT
Juvenile Division

In the Matter of	)	No. 97,643

In the Matter of   )   *No. 97,643*
    Sweeny children   ) DISPOSITION AND ORDER

The above entitled matter having been heard on the *22nd* day of *May 1969,* upon the petition of *Mr. James Elledge* praying that an investigation be made of the circumstances concerning the above named minors, the following persons being present at the hearing: *Patrick and Fern Sweeny, parents; Jack, Dennis, Keith and Robert Sweeny, the children; Attorney Roy Elkins; Deputy District Attorney Michael Hitchman; witnesses.*

and it appearing to the Court, and the Court finding that:

1. Due notice of this proceeding has been given all persons interested herein.

2. The minor is a citizen of this county and under the jurisdiction of the Court.

The Court being fully advised in the premises:

NOW THEREFORE IT IS HEREBY ADJUDGED AND ORDERED:

1. The evidence presented here would indicate that Jack Sweeny is no longer under parental control; therefore, he is to be placed under the jurisdiction of the Welfare Department for foster home placement.

2. Dennis, Keith, and Robert Sweeny are to remain in their parents' home under the supervision of the Welfare Department.

Dated this *23rd* day of *May 1969.*

/S/ Richard Havens
_____
Judge

Jack was placed in a foster home in the Greenleaf School District; arrangements were made for him to be enrolled in the district's behavior modification class. Initially Jack was troublesome. When his foster parents asked him to do tasks around the home, he stood motionless as if he had not heard them. When they pointed out that any privileges he was to receive depended on his behavior, he grudgingly acquiesced to the new system and in a few days was behaving more acceptably.

When he reported to his new school he was boisterous and within the first few minutes had pushed, punched, and shoved several other boys, tickled two of the girls, and asked the teacher how soon they would have recess. Under the rigid control exercised in this special class, Jack soon became less active and started to work for the awards that were offered for good achievement. For the first time he actually made an effort to learn and his skills in traditional academic subjects such as reading, arithmetic, spelling, and social studies improved enormously. He became quite interested in some current world problems and formed a committee under his leadership to welcome new children who were being bussed to the school from black neighborhoods.

He seemed to be making an excellent adjustment, but after a month ran away. His foster parents were alarmed when he missed supper and notified the police and the Juvenile Court counselor. Jack returned to his foster home at 3 a.m. He was cold and tired, and he asked his foster parents to forgive him. His explanation was simple: "I worry every day about my brothers. It's kind of hard to live at home with my dad and mom, and I wonder if my brothers are getting enough to eat or what's happening to them. I made up my mind I would run away and get them to run away with me, and we would go somewhere where we could make it on our own. After I walked away I realized that we would just get arrested again, so I went down under a railroad bridge and sat and thought and thought. I finally decided the best thing to do was for me to come back here and try to get along and try to get through school. That way, when I get older, I can get a good job and take care of my brothers right."

After this, Jack presented no more problems and became a model student in the behavior modification class. But it was difficult to do because his father continually attempted to get him to run away. Mr. Sweeny would sit in his car in the vicinity of Jack's foster home and when he saw Jack would try to talk him into running away or to come home or do something similar, "to show that you love your father." Fortunately Jack resisted, and Sweeny was cautioned that if he persisted he would be subject to arrest and conviction for contempt of court.

Sweeny continued to brood about Jack and the injustice he believed was perpetrated on him by a vindictive society, one that was interested only in taking his son from him. Despite the fact that the younger children continued to steal and misbehave, Mr. Sweeny believed Jack's place was with his parents.

He received two unexpected, lucrative business contracts and found that he was now able to hire a competent attorney to represent him in his quest to regain custody of his son. The attorney was Glen Curry, who was the county chairman of the dominant political party. A petition was filed with the court to have Jack returned to his father's custody. A hearing was held on December 1, 1971, with Mr. Curry representing the parents and with Deputy District Attorney Harry Fields representing the state. Mr. Elledge, the Juvenile Court counselor, was not notified that the hearing was to take place, nor were Jack's foster parents or his teachers. It was held privately and quickly concluded.

STATE CIRCUIT COURT
Juvenile Division

In the Matter of   )   *No. 98,226*
  Jack Sweeny   ) DISPOSITION AND ORDER

The above entitled matter having been heard on the *1st* day of *December 1971,* upon the petition of *Patrick Sweeny* praying that an investigation be made of the circumstances concerning the above named minor, the following persons being present at the hearing: *Patrick and Fern Sweeny, parents; Jack Sweeny, minor son; Mr. Glen Curry, attorney; Deputy District Attorney Harry Fields.*

and it appearing to the Court, and the Court finding that:

1. Due notice of this proceeding has been given all persons interested herein.

2. The minor is a citizen of this county and under the jurisdiction of the Court.

The Court being fully advised in the premises:
NOW THEREFORE IT IS HEREBY ADJUDGED
AND ORDERED:

    1. The evidence presented indicates that Jack Sweeny has now learned to avoid the delinquent behavior that has disrupted this family for so many years, and he is ordered returned to his parents' home.
    2. The wardship is vacated.

Dated this *2nd* day of *December 1971.*

            /S/ Robert Cochran
                    Judge

After the hearing Mr. Curry joked with the deputy district attorney about the judge. "That old bastard knows better than to rule against me," he said. "He knows damn well if he turns down any petition of mine, he will not be reappointed."

Two weeks after Jack was returned to his father's home, Mr. Sweeny became angry because of the behavior of one of the younger boys and announced that none of the children were to be fed for the next week. Jack, in turn, became angry and insulting to his father. He rummaged through his mother's clothes and found two stockings from which he made a mask. He hitchhiked downtown and found a novelty store that sold water pistols which looked remarkably like real automatics. He bought one, then roamed the streets until he found a car with the keys in it. He stole the car and drove to a park, where he waited until it was dark.

That night he held up two gas stations, obtaining $183. He drove to his home neighborhood and parked the stolen car two blocks from his house. He took a ladder from the garage and used it to crawl in the bedroom window. He woke his three brothers, showed them the money he had, and persuaded them to run away with him.

They drove all night and at dawn were arrested in Fort Wayne, Indiana. They told the arresting officers that they were driving their parents' car and that they were going to Chicago to meet their mother and father. The police were skeptical and held the boys in custody. After two days the youngest boy, Robert, began to cry. He told the police his real name and the address of his parents. He said Jack had gotten them to run away and that they were going to Chicago to join the Mafia.

The three youngest sons were returned to the Sweeny home and Jack was brought back to his home town and placed in the custody of the Juvenile Court. A hearing was held on January 4, 1972, Judge Robert Cochran again presiding. Ronald Gleim was appointed to represent Jack. The deputy district attorney was Roger Doppler.

STATE CIRCUIT COURT
Juvenile Division

In the Matter of   )   *No. 99,194*
   Jack Sweeny   )   DISPOSITION AND ORDER

The above entitled matter having been heard on the *1st* day of *January 1972,* upon the petition of *Police Department* praying that an investigation be made of the circumstances concerning the above named minor, the following persons being present at the hearing: *Jack Sweeny, accused; Patrick and Fern Sweeny, parents; Deputy District Attorney Roger Doppler; Attorney Ronald Gleim; witnesses.*

and it appearing to the Court, and the Court finding that:

1. Due notice of this proceeding has been given all persons interested herein.

2. The minor is a citizen of this county and under the jurisdiction of the Court.

The Court being fully advised in the premises:
NOW THEREFORE IT IS HEREBY ADJUDGED
AND ORDERED:

1. Jack Sweeny is to be placed in the custody of the Boys' Industrial Home until he reaches the age of 18, or until such time as that institution deems him to be rehabilitated.

Dated this *2nd* day of *January 1972.*

                     /S/ Robert Cochran
                                  Judge

In the post-trial discussion Judge Cochran saw no irony in the sentence he had pronounced. He was oblivious to the fact that his previous decision to return Jack to his parents' home was directly related to the crime Jack had just committed.

Jack is presently confined in the Boys' Industrial Home where he is an indifferent student in the formal classes held there, but he is very active in learning how to be a good thief and burglar from the more experienced inmates.

Chapter 7 SANDY

Even though Sandy is not my daughter, I'm going to see that she is raised right. I won't permit sin or sinful clothes or music in my house. If I have to beat her to death, I'm going to keep her on the right path, God's path.

—*A stepmother's comment*

Sandy Buhman was a tall, attractive girl who seemed much older than 15 years. She was president of her sophomore class in high school and was very popular. She was an excellent student, and her grades in science courses were outstanding. She hoped to become a physician or a biochemist.

But Sandy's life at home was neither attractive nor excellent nor full of potential. Her new stepmother, who hated her, berated Sandy for an unending succession of imagined wrongs. Not knowing what to do, Sandy discussed her problems with a favorite teacher and was advised to go to the Juvenile Court and ask for help.

Sandy was very calm and reasonable when she went to the court and complained that she was being subjected to harsh, unreasonable discipline by her stepmother. She said she could no longer live at home and asked that she be taken into the Children's Place of Detention until a place for her in a foster home could be found.

In discussing her request with the intake counselor, Sandy said:

I believe that I now am as intelligent as I ever will be, and I hope that I don't get any bigger. I am able to regulate my own affairs, and I am quite willing to abide by any reasonable rules that my father makes. My mother died four years ago, and I still miss her, but everything was fine at home until dad remarried six weeks ago. Eva, the woman dad married, is a real religious nut, and I think she has all

105

kinds of hangups about sex. She is trying to make me wear dresses that are way below my knees, and she has forbidden me the right to have dates or to go to any parties. She keeps warning dad about all the trouble that girls can get into and continues to pester him with ideas that I'm having sex with boys, taking drugs, or smoking pot.

All of her fears are nonsense. I work hard in school, and I am a good student with nearly all A's. I have dates with boys and there are two or three that I like very much, but nothing serious. I kiss boys once in a while, but I'm still a virgin and intend to stay that way for quite a while. I'm not a bad girl, and I never get in trouble, but I can't stand it at home.

Last night I stopped on my way home from school and had a coke with a friend of mine. As a result, I was half an hour late getting home from school. Eva really blew her stack and accused me of being in bed with some man. She took an old yardstick that's been lying around the house and attempted to beat me with it. It was a silly, hysterical scene. I'm much bigger and stronger than she is, and I wasn't about to stand there and let her hit me, so I took the yardstick away from her. She continued to scream and holler at me, and then ran over to our nearest neighbor's house. The windows were open, and I could hear her in their house screaming about what a bad girl I was. It was very embarrassing.

That night when dad got home from work, Eva told him that I had been in bed with a boy, and she insisted that he punish me. Dad has never spanked me in his life, and he didn't know how, but he did ground me for a month. I told him that I had done nothing wrong, and I asked him if he believed what Eva had told him. He said he didn't know, and that really hurt me to realize that my dad could be turned against me by a nutty woman like that.

I want to be placed in some foster home. It doesn't have to be anything fancy—just any kind of ordinary home will be fine, and I will behave. I am not going to live in my home any more, and if my father or the courts insist that I go back home, I'll just run away, but next time I won't do it legally. I'll make it on my own and live underground. I want to do it the right way, but if I can't, I'll do it any way I can.

Sandy was taken into custody and her father and stepmother were notified as to her whereabouts. They immediately came to the agency, and Mrs. Buhman became so belligerent that it was necessary to call the police.

DEPARTMENT OF PUBLIC SAFETY
BUREAU OF POLICE
Officer's Report

1. Specific Crime	2. Place of Occurrence	3. Case No.
Public Disturbance	Juvenile Court House	43,971

4. Date and Time Crime Occurred	5. Date and Time Crime Reported
Oct. 23, 1969 Approximately 11:00 AM	Oct. 23, 1969 Approximately 11:15 AM

6. Victim's Name	7. Person Reporting Crime
None	Elizabeth Sonnenbrock Juvenile Court Social Worker

8. Witnesses' Names	9. Suspect(s) Name
Harry Foley, Juvenile Court Jane Stacey, Juvenile Court Elizabeth Sonnenbrock, Juvenile Court	Eva Buhman 4198 Parkridge Terrace

10. Narrative of Crime, Describe Evidence, Summarize Details Not Given Above.

At about 11:15 AM writer received 219 from Radio Division. Proceeded to Juvenile Court and was met by Mrs. Sonnenbrock who took me to area where commotion was occurring. A woman identified as Mrs. Eva Buhman was screaming that she was being persecuted by agents of the devil. Her husband was attempting to calm her. Harry Foley and Jane Stacey said they had been trying to calm her for some time, but that she seemed insane.

Spoke to Mrs. Buhman and advised her that her behavior constituted a crime for which she could be arrested, and that unless she calmed down I

would be forced to take her to police station. She
quieted down, but indicated that I was part of some
plot to persecute her.

None of those present were willing to prefer
charges so arrest not made. Believe Mrs. Buhman
may be insane, but did not seem to present danger to
self or others.

$$/S/ \ \text{Peter Rich}$$
Badge No. 4732
Day Relief

A preliminary hearing was held on October 29, 1969. The
referee, Alex Burden, ruled that Sandy be given a psychological evaluation and that an investigation be made as to
the fitness of the Buhman home.

Walter Bullard, Ph.D., a psychologist at the County Mental Health Out-Patient Clinic, was assigned to evaluate
Sandy. He interviewed and tested her on November 4 and
made his report to the Juvenile Court.

COUNTY DEPARTMENT OF PUBLIC HEALTH
MENTAL HEALTH OUT-PATIENT CLINIC
(963) 432-1122   763 Fourth Ave. N.W.

Robert Grednoe, M.D., Director

November 6, 1969

Mrs. Wanda Spano
Juvenile Court Counselor
Children's Place of Detention

Dear Mrs. Spano:
   Sandy Buhman was referred to me for an evaluation by
your agency. It is my understanding that this attractive, 15-
year-old, Caucasian girl has refused to remain in her father's
home and is seeking refuge at your agency from the abusive
behavior of her stepmother, Eva Buhman.

Sandy was interviewed and tested by me on November 4, 1969. The test results indicate that her present level of intellectual functioning is in the superior range, with a Full Scale IQ of 138, a Performance IQ of 135, and a Verbal IQ of 141. There was very little variance between the sub-test scores, and it was apparent that this was an extremely gifted young lady.

A battery of personality tests was administered, and it appeared that Sandy's test-taking attitude was one of normal defensiveness. The results would indicate that she was free from any pathological anxiety, depression, or agitation. There was no evidence of any mood or thought disorder. In essence, she appeared to be a normal, well-adjusted girl of superior intelligence.

At the conclusion of the testing session we discussed Sandy's reasons for leaving her father's home. She described her stepmother, Eva, as being a very rigid, uncompromising woman, who was attempting to impose religious dogma on Sandy to an abnormal degree, and Sandy stated that she refused to accept this treatment any longer.

I have not had an opportunity to interview Mrs. Buhman, and I have no way of ascertaining the accuracy of Sandy's statements. However, I am convinced that Sandy believes the situation that she described to be true and that if she is forced to return to Mrs. Buhman's control, she will run away. I firmly believe that she will carry out her threat, and I would be most fearful as to the results. She is an extremely attractive girl, but despite her intelligence, she is completely inexperienced in many of the more sordid aspects of our community, and I would fear that she might become a part of the drug culture or that she might be victimized by other unscrupulous individuals.

I would strongly recommend that she be placed in a foster home and that her father be given full visitation rights. If Sandy is ever to return to her home, it might be desirable to recommend to Mr. and Mrs. Buhman that they receive counseling in child rearing practices.

In conclusion, I would reiterate that Sandy will not submit to her stepmother's domination, and that if an attempt is made to force her to live with her stepmother, she will most certainly run away.

Very truly yours,

/S/ Walter Bullard, Ph.D.
Clinical Psychologist

Mrs. Elizabeth Sonnenbrock, a social worker at the Juvenile Court, made an investigation of the Buhman home. She found the home to be extremely neat and clean and very tastefully furnished. Both Mr. and Mrs. Buhman were home when she called. Mr. Buhman expressed appropriate concern for his daughter and suggested that if she were allowed to return to their home, that they would try to be less harsh in their treatment of her.

Mrs. Buhman refused to agree to adopt a more lenient attitude and stated repeatedly that Sandy must be made to behave. When inquiry was made as to specific instances of Sandy's misbehavior, Mrs. Buhman simply stated that "she's into all sorts of things and all she has on her mind is sex. She wants to wear them short dresses and run around with boys, but that's the road to sin, and I am going to save her."

The neighbors reported that Mr. Buhman had always been a quiet, good neighbor, but that since his recent marriage, there seemed to be much discord in the home and that Mrs. Buhman was a frequent visitor to their homes. During these visits Mrs. Buhman exhorted them to change their ways and follow God's way. Apparently none of the neighbors had Mrs. Buhman's highly developed sense of sin, for they considered her to be an annoying eccentric.

A final hearing to adjudicate the problem was held on December 2, 1969. Judge Chester Beshaw presided. Present were Mr. and Mrs. Buhman, Sandy; Mr. Richard Trapp, attorney for the parents; Mrs. Sonnenbrock of the Juvenile Court; Dr. Bullard; and Raymond Hazel, deputy district attorney.

STATE CIRCUIT COURT
Juvenile Division

In the Matter of	)	No. 96,447
Sandy Buhman, minor	)	DISPOSITION AND ORDER

The above entitled matter having been heard on the *2nd* day of *December 1969,* upon the petition of *Mrs. Sonnenbrock, social worker* praying that an investigation be made of the circumstances concerning the above named minor, the following persons being present at the hearing: *Frank and Eva Buhman, parents; Sandy Buhman, minor child; Mr. Richard Trapp, Attorney; Mr. Raymond Hazel, Deputy District Attorney; witnesses.*

and it appearing to the Court, and the Court finding that:

1. Due notice of this proceeding has been given all persons interested herein.

2. The minor is a citizen of this county and under the jurisdiction of the Court.

The Court being fully advised in the premises:
NOW THEREFORE IT IS HEREBY ADJUDGED
AND ORDERED:

    1. Evidence presented would indicate that Mr. and Mrs. Buhman maintain a good Christian home and that Sandy Buhman has not been the victim of abuse or neglect.

    2. Sandy Buhman is ordered released from the jurisdiction of this court and returned to her parents' custody.

Dated this *3rd* day of *December 1969.*

                    /S/ Chester Beshaw
                    ————————————————
                              Judge

Two days after she was returned home Sandy prepared to run away. She canvassed all of her friends and managed to borrow $25. That night she packed a small suitcase and quietly left home. She went to the bus station, intending to catch a bus for a nearby city. She was unpleasantly surprised when she learned the amount of the bus fare and realized that after paying it she would have very little money left when she arrived. She decided to sit down and think about the best course to follow.

While she was trying to decide what to do, a handsome young man, John Spielman, approached her and told her he was bored and lonesome and wondered if she cared to "rap" with him. Sandy was somewhat hesitant, but after a few minutes she began to discuss her problems with him. He was very sympathetic. Finally he suggested that they have a drink in a nearby bar. Sandy was thrilled. For the first time in her life she was being treated as an adult by an adult, and it was flattering to realize that she was attractive to a man like John.

After a few drinks she was happy and hilarious. She spent the night in John's bed. Sandy became attached to her newfound lover and reveled in her freedom as an adult. She eagerly followed any suggestion that was made to her and was soon experimenting with pot and narcotics. She was frequently intoxicated.

John worked as a bartender and insisted that Sandy keep out of the bar. So it was something of a surprise when he phoned one night and asked her to come to the bar. When she arrived, he motioned her to the end of the bar and whispered, "Look, Sandy, we're short of money, and there is no reason why you can't turn a couple tricks and make us some quick heavy bread." Sandy was not sure what he meant, and he explained. "See that old guy at the end of the bar? He's been looking for a girl all night, and he'll pay $100. Go up and talk to him and go home with him and do whatever he wants. I'll collect from him before he leaves."

Sandy protested, but John quietly told her that she would have to do what he said or he would turn her in for being a runaway and for using narcotics. "It's up to you, kid. You'll do what I say or go to jail." As an afterthought he also threatened to beat her if she did not do as he asked. Reluctantly Sandy became a whore. Three months later she was arrested.

DEPARTMENT OF PUBLIC SAFETY
BUREAU OF POLICE
Officer's Report

1. Specific Crime	2. Place of Occurrence	3. Case No.
Prostitution	Great Northern Hotel 211 N. Bear St.	54,991

4. Date and Time Crime Occurred	5. Date and Time Crime Reported
April 11, 1970, at 1:15 AM	Not applicable

6. Victim's Name	7. Person Reporting Crime
None	Writer

8. Witnesses' Names	9. Suspect(s) Name
Writer	Sandy Buhman, age 15 Great Northern Hotel, Rm 817

10. Narrative of Crime, Describe Evidence, Summarize Details Not Given Above.

At 12:30 AM writer entered the bar of the Great Northern Hotel on routine vice patrol. Ordered drink and was approached by suspect who asked if writer was having a good time. Told her I was. She asked if I would like to have a party and I asked what kind of party. Suspect said I could have a straight lay for $25.00, but that anything else would cost $40.00

Went to Room 817 with suspect. She examined writer's genitals for veneral disease and accepted

11. Continuation of Officer's Report

$25.00. Arrest made at this time. Advised suspect
of rights and she refused to make any statement,
said friends would get attorney and free her.
Learned suspect was minor and took her to Children's
Place of Detention.

> /S/ Herbert Ruether
> Badge No. 2143
> Vice and Narcotic Detail

Because Sandy was a juvenile the hearing was held in
Juvenile Court. Judge Chester Beshaw presided at the preliminary hearing. He argued that Sandy should be immediately remanded to an adult court for trial and stated that
the girl was an obvious degenerate. However, Mrs. Sonnenbrock requested that a psychiatric evaluation be made, and
the judge reluctantly agreed. Sandy was examined by Dr.
Leslie Spies, who reported:

> This 16-year-old girl has recently been involved in a drasti-
> cally anti-social life of prostitution. It would be my opinion
> that Sandy does not have a sociopathic or anti-social per-
> sonality, but that to a very large extent she was a victim of
> circumstances, trapped between two equally repugnant al-
> ternatives. As she saw her situation, she had the choice of
> either going to jail for an indeterminant period of time or
> resorting to prostitution. She chose the latter.
> Examination does not reveal any evidence of neurotic or
> psychotic tendencies, and she appears to be appropriately
> repentent for her behavior. She is anxious to be placed in a
> foster home and to return to high school. Certainly a girl
> with this intelligence belongs in school rather than in jail or
> on the streets.
> I believe Sandy to be highly salvageable, and I would
> strongly recommend that she be placed in a foster home and
> encouraged to return to school. I would be very fearful of
> her future if she were sentenced to jail and exposed to the
> malignant influence of other women inmates.

Judge Beshaw was unmoved by the psychiatrist's report. When the final hearing was held, he remanded Sandy to an adult court. Her parents refused to hire an attorney to represent her; an attorney was appointed by the court. The attorney was an experienced criminal attorney. He reached a compromise with the district attorney which provided that Sandy would spend only six weeks in jail. He considered this a legal victory, and Sandy reluctantly agreed to plead guilty and accept the light sentence.

During her confinement in jail, Sandy was continuously exposed to a group of extremely deviant women. She suffered two homosexual assaults and was involved in several fights.

On completion of her sentence, Sandy was released to the juvenile authorities. They returned her to the custody of her father and stepmother, and she escaped that night. Her present whereabouts are unknown.

Chapter 8 DAVID

> I had to stop him from talking to his father because I couldn't
> be sure what he would say. I was always afraid he would
> mention one of the other men, so I whipped him and made
> him stop talking except when he and I were alone. I told his
> father he was sick and that I was taking him to a doctor.
>
> *—A mother's statement*

Rex and Ann Glasgow had the most handsome house on
the street. Rex Glasgow was a competent, successful industrial engineer, and his services were so highly valued by
his employer that he received frequent salary increases.
Rex reciprocated by devoting more and more time and
energy to his job and frequently worked 12 hours a day.
He and Ann had been married six years and had a five-
year-old son, David.

As Rex became more and more involved with his job, his
relationship with his wife and son deteriorated. He seldom
arrived home before nine in the evening and then had time
only for dinner before going to bed. Yet despite the minimal contact with his son, Rex was worried about him.
David did not seem to be able to talk. Ann said she had
taken David to the best doctors in town. She assured Rex
that he was getting good treatment, but Rex was still concerned. He often wished he could spend more time with
the boy.

Rex and Ann had many friends but held themselves aloof
from their neighbors, with whom they had little contact.
David was seldom seen and was never permitted to play
with any of the other children in the neighborhood.

The neighbors, being neighbors, were curious—and a bit
jealous. They noticed that numerous men frequently vis-

ited the Glasgow home when Rex was at work, and it was assumed throughout the neighborhood that Ann was having affairs with these men.

The assumptions were correct. Ann had become increasingly isolated from her husband. In a search for affection and companionship she had become increasingly involved with other men. She had become wanton in her behavior and frequently had sexual intercourse with several men in a period of one week.

David was an impediment to Ann's extramarital affairs. When he was 21 months old he called one of her lovers "Dada." She grew afraid that as he learned to talk, he would give clues to Rex that she was having affairs. She determined to keep the boy from ever talking to his father. As his early speech developed, she succeeded in training him to talk only when they were alone together. Rex was told that David had a malformed throat which prevented him from talking, and Ann became skilled at describing fictitious interviews with imagined throat specialists. Rex was allowed to hope that David would develop normal vocal skills, but he was cautioned to be patient.

One night screams were heard coming from the Glasgow home, and the neighbors called the police.

DEPARTMENT OF PUBLIC SAFETY
BUREAU OF POLICE
Officer's Report

1. Specific Crime	2. Place of Occurrence	3. Case No.
Assault	3665 N.E. Pasadena	70-294

4. Date and Time Crime Occurred	5. Date and Time Crime Reported
Nov. 18, 1968 at app. 9:30 PM	Nov. 18, 1968 at 9:40 PM

6. Victim's Name	7. Person Reporting Crime
Ann Glasgow, 3665 N.E. Pasadena	Harriet Autry 3659 N.E. Pasadena
8. Witnesses' Names None	9. Suspect(s) Name Rex Glasgow (Husband) 3665 N.E. Pasadena

10. Narrative of Crime, Describe Evidence, Summarize Details Not Given Above.

Received 219 at 9:45 above date and proceeded to Pasadena Ave. address. Suspect admitted writer to premises. Explained to suspect that writer had reason to believe that someone in house had been screaming. Suspect stated "that was my wife, the no good bitch." Suspect further stated that wife had lied to him about their son and he had beaten her with his fists and with a mop handle. At this point writer stopped suspect and fully advised him on his rights. Suspect said he did not want an attorney present and that he did not care if he was arrested. Suspect also said that he was glad that he had beaten his wife, and that he would do it again if given chance.

Suspect took writer to kitchen of Pasadena address where Ann Glasgow was found. Victim had numerous cuts and contusions on face, arms and legs. Victim was conscious, and did not appear groggy or confused. Writer offered to call ambulance, but victim refused, said could get to hospital on her own.

Suspect said altercation occurred because he came home early and entered rear of house unknown to victim and found victim and son David (age 5) talking. Suspect said he had been told son could not talk, and he realized that victim had lied to him for years. Said tried to beat truth out of victim and that victim confessed to having affairs with

11. Continuation of Officer's Report

other men, and stopped son from talking to suspect
so that he would not learn truth. Victim agreed that
this is what happened and that she did not blame
suspect. Asked victim if she desired to prefer
charges, and she said that she did not, so no arrest
made.

> /S/ Jack Martin
> Badge No. 8971
> 1st Nite Relief

After this incident Rex was distraught. He could not
tolerate Ann's presence. Ann agreed to leave the home and
seek psychiatric care. Rex kept David and arranged for him
to be seen at a child guidance clinic.

Ann got an appointment with Dr. Leslie Dodge, a psychiatrist. In making notes of his first interview with Ann,
Dr. Dodge wrote:

> This patient was interviewed for the first time on Decem-
> ber 20, 1968. She is an extremely attractive girl who was
> dressed in quiet good taste. Her posture and mannerisms
> were appropriate to the occasion. She did not manifest any
> signs of distress or anxiety, remaining calm and controlled
> throughout the interview.
> Her speech was very precise, and she articulated so care-
> fully that she appeared to be speaking with an unfamiliar
> accent. Her voice was low and well modulated. She was
> properly oriented as to time, place and person, and her as-
> sociation of ideas followed a logical progression. Her level of
> intelligence appeared to be within normal limits, and she
> appeared able to recall recent and remote events with ease.
> She did not report experiencing hallucinations, but she was
> concerned with the delusion that she sometimes experienced
> that people could read her mind.
> Her mood appeared somber and depressed. She stated that
> she had no goals, that she was evil and worthless, and that
> her entire life had been wasted. She felt alienated from peo-

ple; felt that no one ever had or ever would love her; and that she was a sex-ridden hag. She was extremely guilty over her treatment of her son, David, and expressed great remorse over her behavior toward him.

This patient is the youngest of two sisters, and she also has a step-sister and a step-brother who are the results of her mother's second marriage. Her father was an alcoholic and her parents were divorced when she was two. Her mother and the two girls then lived with her mother's parents until the patient graduated from high school at which time she moved to this city to attend a secretarial college. She was an average student in school, but she feels that she never really tried to obtain good grades.

She has always felt that she was a person of little worth and that her life was drab and uneventful. Since early adolescence she has attempted to enhance herself by pretence, telling her friends and family outrageous lies involving romantic adventures and tragic loves. She is frightened because she is aware that she sometimes believes these lies after she has repeated them frequently.

She is appalled at her sexual behavior and recalls her first sexual involvement when she was about four years old. At that time a man frequently had her sit in his car, and he persuaded her to fondle his genitals. As a reward she would receive candy. As a child she engaged in the usual investigatory activities as well as an attempted act of bestiality, but the dog would not cooperate. She experienced true heterosexual relations with her cousins and others while in high school and estimated that she has been intimate with perhaps 400 men since that time. She experiences an orgasm only through masturbation. She denies any homosexual experiences or feelings. While engaging in sexual activities she remains aloof and wary and never permits herself to become truly affectionate toward her lovers. She has never learned or conceived of alternate methods that she might employ to gain the love and affection that she desires. She believes that only during the sexual act is she esteemed and wanted.

In discussing her behavior toward her son she explained that she lived in dread of the day that he would tell her husband of the parade of men that were visiting the home and little by little she found herself training the boy never to speak in the presence of his father. She succeeded in keeping the boy isolated and deprived him of most of the learning experiences so necessary in infancy and early childhood. She pretended to be worried about the boy's speech development when she discussed this matter with her husband and repeatedly assured her husband that David was receiving adequate medical care. She is truly appalled about her behavior and believes that she must be insane.

This patient has many areas of strength, including her normal level of intelligence, her ability to distinguish reality from fantasy, her realization that she alone is the source of her problems, and her apparent sincere and earnest desire to modify her behavior.

Rex Glasgow was disturbed at the events that had occurred. He had thought of himself as being highly successful both as an engineer and as a husband. The realization that his wife had been so flagrantly unfaithful caused him to question not only his own success, but many of his established beliefs and values. "If I can be so wrong in this," he thought, "how can I be sure I am right in anything?"

David presented serious problems. He had been inhibited from speaking to his father and denied normal living experiences for so long that his freedom was frightening to him. A former teacher was employed to act as a babysitter while Rex was working. Under this tutelage David advanced rapidly, but he became a noisy exuberant boy, and his play and loud shrieks annoyed Rex when he was home.

Gradually Rex began to toy with the notion that this pesky child was not his own. In view of the frequency with which Ann had had intercourse with other men, it seemed reasonable to suppose that her pregnancy might have been the result of an extramarital adventure instead of by sexual intercourse with him. Subconsciously the notion that the boy was not his own was very appealing to Rex, for if David were another man's son, Rex could hardly be responsible for his care and education.

Rex consulted with his family physician to determine if there were blood tests or other laboratory procedures that might be undertaken to determine if he were really David's father. He was disappointed to learn that there were no tests that would conclusively demonstrate that another man was responsible.

Rex confronted Ann and demanded that she be honest with him and tell him if David were really his son. Still depressed, as well as defenseless, Ann readily conceded that she did not know if Rex or one of several men had fathered the boy.

David irritated Rex more and more. He became a symbol of Ann's infidelity and Rex's blind stupidity in trusting her. One evening when David was being particularly noisy, Rex lost his temper and beat the boy violently. After he calmed down, Rex, now frightened by his behavior, rushed with the boy to a physician. He freely admitted that he was the one who had beaten David. While the physician could not detect any serious injury, he strongly advised Rex to have the boy hospitalized for a few days. He also advised Rex that he had to report the matter to the police. Rex concurred and agreed to put David in the hospital.

After David's release from the hospital the Juvenile Court placed him in the Wilson Shelter for Children. The Juvenile Affairs Bureau petitioned the court to have David made a ward of the court and placed in a foster home. Mr. and Mrs. Glasgow were both aware of their pathological behavior in their feelings toward David; therefore they did not contest the decision. As a result, David was made a ward of the court and placed under the jurisdiction of the Welfare Department which placed him in a foster home. Arrangements were made for special education classes, and David was seen in play therapy at a child guidance agency.

The results of this changed environment and of the play therapy were gratifying. David became a happy, well-adjusted boy able to function well in his foster home and in school. Both parents had visitation rights, but they seldom took advantage of them and saw very little of David.

During the following year Ann and Rex were divorced. Ann remained in therapy with Dr. Dodge, and Rex made generous contributions to her support. He also paid the full cost of David's foster home and for the special educational measures that had been undertaken. Ann and Rex met each other occasionally; it was apparent to both of them that they were still strongly attracted to one another. But Rex's feelings toward Ann were mixed. He thought of her as likable and attractive, but he also hated her for the deception that had occurred. Despite this, in a mellow moment, they decided to remarry.

After several weeks of marriage they began to feel that all of their problems had been resolved. They decided they wanted David returned to their home. They engaged attorney Paul Kneeland to represent them and petitioned the court for custody of David. Ann permitted Dr. Dodge to testify as to her emotional stability, and Rex voluntarily underwent an examination by Dr. Douglas, a psychologist appointed by the court. A hearing was held on April 7, 1970, with Judge Mary Osborne presiding. The parents were represented by Mr. Kneeland, and the deputy district attorney was Mr. Stephen Pitzer. Drs. Dodge and Douglas were the only witnesses.

Dr. Dodge testified that he had seen Ann twice each week for the past year. During that period she had become quite free in discussing her feelings and emotions, but she remained severely depressed and puzzled by her previous behavior. She claimed that she had been able to stifle her sexual impulses and that her promiscuity had abated, but she found that she continued to use men in a variety of ways. Apparently she was quite interested in the men she met until it became apparent that this interest was reciprocated; then she became irritated and intolerant of them. Apparently her feelings of guilt and self-contempt generated a high degree of anger, which she externalized toward many of those with whom she was in contact. She remained suspicious of and sensitive to the opinions of others and continuously suspected other people of being hostile and inconsiderate toward her. Her level of anxiety was so high that she was presently operating at a fairly low intellectual level. She confined her reading to magazines such as *True Story* and found many movies difficult to understand. She exhibited overconcern about trivial matters and tended to react to minor irritations as if they were major emergencies. She would be capable of gross outbursts of anger, and at times was capable of being physically assaultive.

Dr. Dodge concluded his testimony by stating that he believed Ann was presently not capable of caring for David adequately, and recommended that the child remain in the foster home.

Dr. Douglas testified that Rex was a man of superior intelligence who was not suffering from any psychosis or thought disorder. Douglas thought, however, that Rex had highly conflicting feelings about his wife and that it was a strong love-hate relationship. In view of Rex's previous abusive treatment of David, Dr. Douglas was fearful that this would be repeated and strongly recommended that the child not be returned to the Glasgows.

STATE CIRCUIT COURT
Juvenile Division

| In the Matter of |) | *No. 73,990* |
| *David Glasgow, minor* |) | DISPOSITION AND ORDER |

The above entitled matter having been heard on the *7th* day of *April 1970,* upon the petition of *Rex and Ann Glasgow*

praying that an investigation be made of the circumstances
concerning the above named minor, the following persons
being present at the hearing: *Rex and Ann Glasgow, parents;
David Glasgow, minor; Attorney Paul Kneeland; Deputy
Attorney Stephen Pitzer; witnesses.*

and it appearing to the Court, and the Court finding that:
   1. Due notice of this proceeding has been given all persons
interested herein.
   2. The minor is a citizen of this county and under the jurisdiction of the Court.

The Court being fully advised in the premises:
NOW THEREFORE IT IS HEREBY ADJUDGED
AND ORDERED:

   *The testimony offered here would indicate that Mr. and Mrs.
Glasgow have made serious constructive efforts to resolve
their personal and marital problems. It is ordered:*

   1. David Glasgow will continue as a ward of this court.
   *2. He will be returned to the custody of his parents under
the supervision of the Welfare Department.*

Dated this *8th* day of *April 1970.*

                         /S/ Mary Osborne
                         _____
                                        Judge

   During a routine visit by the welfare worker, David was
found with a blackened eye and cut lip. He said that his
father had hit him, but both Rex and Ann denied this. On
a subsequent visit, the boy was again found to be bruised
and appeared to have regressed psychologically, in that he
was no longer talking much. The Welfare Department petitioned the court to remove David from his parents' custody, but Judge Paul Ivan refused to intervene.

STATE CIRCUIT COURT
Juvenile Division

| In the Matter of |) | *No. 74,178* |
| *David Glasgow, minor* |) | DISPOSITION AND ORDER |

The above entitled matter having been heard on the *10th* day of *December 1970,* upon the petition of *Welfare Department* praying that an investigation be made of the circumstances concerning the above named minor, the following persons being present at the hearing: *Rex and Ann Glasgow, parents; David Glasgow, minor; Attorney Paul Kneeland; Deputy District Attorney Stephen Pitzer; witnesses.*

and it appearing to the Court, and the Court finding that:

1. Due notice of this proceeding has been given all persons interested herein.

2. The minor is a citizen of this county and under the jurisdiction of the Court.

The Court being fully advised in the premises:
NOW THEREFORE IT IS HEREBY ADJUDGED
AND ORDERED:

The testimony offered here would indicate that David Glasgow has received some slight physical injuries and that he has experienced learning difficulties, but it has not been shown that this is the result of actions by his parents.

1. David Glasgow will continue as a ward of this court.
2. Custody will remain with his parents under Welfare Department supervision.

Dated this *11th* day of *December 1970.*

/S/ *Paul Ivan*
_____
Judge

The caseload at the Welfare Department was so heavy that visits by a regular social worker were discontinued, and a volunteer worker was found who visited the Glasgow home once a month. She did not report any evidence of child abuse during the next three months, but the school was anxious about David's continuing regression to a primitive level. The boy refused to talk in school, he did not accomplish any of his assignments, and he spent most of his time staring at his hands, quietly humming.

At the insistence of the principal of David's school, another petition was prepared for the court. Rex became irritated and apparently began to believe that he was suffering from some sort of persecution. He found a job in another state and moved his wife and child out of the jurisdiction of the Juvenile Court prior to the date of the hearing. No extradition is possible in such cases. It is assumed that as Rex and Ann continue their love-hate relationship, they will continue the psychological destruction of their child.

Chapter 9 GALE

He knew it made me mad when he cried, but that morning he started crying when he got up and everything that happened made him cry more. I decided to spank him, and he knew he needed one, but he rolled over on his back so I couldn't hit him. I grabbed him by the head and shoulders to try to turn him over to spank him and something broke in his neck and he died.

—A mother's comment

John and Margaret Bentley were quiet, nervous little people who lived in a rather isolated house several miles from the nearest town. Both John and Margaret had had very difficult childhoods and as adolescents were bashful and aloof. They had dated little and had few friends. John was 28 and Margaret was 21 when they met at a church supper. They were drawn together largely because they were ignored by everyone else. They had a few dates and found that they were comfortable with each other. After six months they were married.

John was a successful certified public accountant. He took pleasure in the rhythms of numbers successfully manipulated. His income was large, but he was anxious about money; his fear of poverty was genuine and intense. During their engagement he persuaded Margaret to help him, and they built a house largely with their own labor. They saw it as a wedding present to each other and spent their honeymoon there.

John and Margaret related freely with one another when discussing material things, but it was difficult for either of them to show affection or feeling. John took great pleasure in his growing savings account, while Margaret, being a compulsive person who was overly concerned with neatness and personal cleanliness, thoroughly enjoyed her duties as a housewife.

Their daughter Gale was born after their first year of marriage. Margaret thought Gale was a pleasant, well-behaved child who was content to play quietly alone and who seldom irritated her mother. Their son Roy was born two years later. He was a very active infant; as soon as he was able to crawl, he explored the whole house. In his explorations he frequently knocked ashtrays off tables, spilled glasses, or found other ways to make the house untidy. His mother was continuously annoyed at his behavior. On August 15, 1969, the day before his second birthday, she murdered him.

DEPARTMENT OF PUBLIC SAFETY
BUREAU OF POLICE
Officer's Report

1. Specific Crime Murder	2. Place of Occurrence 17846 Rutgers Road RR #103, Box 27	3. Case No. 70–1933

4. Date and Time Crime Occurred 8/15/69 between 8:30 and 8:45 AM	5. Date and Time Crime Reported 8/15/69 10:05 AM
6. Victim's Name Roy Bentley, male, aged 2	7. Person Reporting Crime Richard Mills, M.D. resident at River Haven Hospital
8. Witnesses' Names Richard Mills, M.D. and Paula Hendge, R.N. both on staff of River Haven Hospital	9. Suspect(s) Name Margaret Bentley, mother of victim

10. Narrative of Crime, Describe Evidence, Summarize Details Not Given Above.

Sgt. Arena received report from Coroner's office stating that there was a dead child at River Haven Hospital that had been killed by its mother. Sgt. Arena assigned case to writer.

Proceeded to River Haven Hospital and was met at emergency entrance by Dr. Richard Mills and Nurse Paula Hendge who advised that victim was a two year old boy who had died of broken neck. Also advised by these two that mother (Margaret Bentley) had confessed to killing victim. Viewed body and noted cuts on face and what appeared to be old bruises on legs and buttocks.

Interviewed Bentley woman and fully advised her of her rights. She said that she would talk to me, that attorney couldn't help her. Suspect said that she was feeling bad and that victim had been upsetting house, pulling things onto floor, and that victim would not stop no matter what she said to him. Said started to spank victim but he rolled over so she could not hit buttocks. Suspect said she then grabbed victim by head to roll him over so she could spank him and something broke in his neck and he died.

Placed suspect, Mrs. Margaret Bentley, under arrest and proceeded to Station for booking and taking of formal statement.

                    /S/ Det. Joseph Streeter
                    Badge No. 5131
                    Day Relief

Following Margaret's arrest the Juvenile Court became concerned about Gale's welfare and ordered her placed in the Wilson Shelter for Children. On admission to the Shelter she was found to be a somber, listless child who was very quiet and appeared to lack spontaneity. Her physical health was good, and there was no evidence of abuse.

John was loyal to his wife despite his son's murder. He hired a well-known attorney, Irving Benz, who decided that the best defense was probably one of temporary insanity. When the nature of the defense was communicated to the district attorney, he exercised his prerogative and ordered that independent evaluations of Mrs. Bentley be made. As a result she was evaluated by a psychiatrist, John Deady, M.D., and by a psychologist, Roger Hartner, Ph.D. Dr. Deady reported:

Mr. John Bentley and Mrs. Margaret Bentley were interviewed on 9/11/69. This woman was anxious, answered questions rapidly and accurately, and appeared to have above average intelligence. There were numerous times when her behavior was inappropriate in that she laughed and giggled for no apparent reason, but I felt that this was because of the tension that she was under. Her immediate and remote memory was intact. I did not detect any evidence of serious depression or any sort of psychosis.

During the interview Mrs. Bentley volunteered that she had always been nervous since she had been forced to have sexual relations with her father for a considerable period of time, and that she can recall becoming quite emotionally upset when this was stopped at about the time she became 18. This woman is particularly preoccupied with the anger she has had toward her mother, both past and present. She stated that she felt her father turned to her sexually because her mother was frigid. It does not appear that she has any anger or ill-will toward her father. Apparently she believes that the whole pathological situation was her mother's fault.

She further stated that her sexual relationships with her father were frequently interrupted by her younger brother's crying, and that whenever he cried, she and her father were fearful that the mother would awake and, therefore, they would terminate their sexual activity. She stated that she knew it was wrong, but that ever since that time the sound of a child crying had made her extremely angry.

In discussing the death of her son, Mrs. Bentley did not display any emotion. She spoke in a flat monotone and described the events as if they were some common every day occurrence.

Mr. Bentley is a rather odd looking man who appears to be well oriented and to have no evidence of depression or psychosis. However, he is an extremely anxious, compulsive sort of individual, and apparently has always had strong neurotic symptoms. He openly stated his anger at the police and the District Attorney for disrupting his home and apparently believes that his wife's murder of their son was simply a mistake that should best be quickly forgotten. He did not express any concern or curiosity about his daughter.

It is my impression that Mrs. Bentley is quite capable of participating in her own defense and that she is free from any psychosis or crippling neuroses that might tend to mitigate her guilt. However, it would be difficult for me to conceive that this couple could function adequately as parents of a child.

Dr. Hartner reported:

Mrs. Bentley is a slender woman who was neatly and appropriately dressed. She was most cooperative, but it was noted that she tended not to make spontaneous decisions and to check on rather minute details when she was responding to the tests that were being administered. She stated that she was much more calm that she had been in the past because of tranquilizers that had been prescribed for her. A minute, fine tremor of the hands was observed which she said had been present since childhood. Her medical history is not significant, and there are no reported episodes of epilepsy, convulsions, black-outs, or periods of unconsciousness. She considers that she has always been in good health except that she has always been "quite nervous."

Mrs. Bentley's family background and developmental history are most malignant. Her father was orphaned at the age of 16, and he was raised by relatives who had extremely poor standards and whose behavior was characterized by illegitimate pregnancies, drunkenness, and arrests for petty crimes. Her mother found school difficult and had dropped out in the fourth grade. Her parents met in Los Angeles, and after a two-month courtship married when the mother was 16 and the father 22. It would appear that they were drawn together by their own unhappy growing up experiences. In the early years of their marriage they were close, but Mrs. Bentley felt that this changed and that her mother discontinued sexual relationships with her father, possibly because of fear of pregnancy.

Mrs. Bentley recalled that when she was about 12 years old, her father began to insist on rubbing her chest with ointment to prevent tuberculosis, and although she demurred, both her mother and father insisted that she submit, and they both laughed at her objections. The intimacy thus initiated developed into a full sexual relationship with her father, lasting for six years. She enjoyed the physical aspects of this and recalled the positive feelings she experienced from her father's tender endearments. In retrospect, she is inclined to believe that her mother must have been aware of this intimacy because of her subsequent comments, but there was no overt mention made of the topic until Mrs. Bentley's husband confronted the mother directly several weeks ago.

Mrs. Bentley stated that she used to daydream a great deal, and she can remember a bitter blow-up on the part of her mother when her report card indicated that she did not make good use of her time. Apparently her mother wanted her to succeed where she, the mother, had not been able to make the grade. She believed that she had never been able to please her mother, and over the years she would hope that some day her mother would give her some recognition or approval. Instead her mother continued to belittle her and criticize her behavior in school and in the home.

In discussing her relationship with her husband she described him as a very rigid man, who conformed in a rather meticulous, rote manner, and who insisted that his life follow a definite pattern. On the first and second night of their marriage he was not able to achieve an erection, and his distress about this and his feelings of guilt triggered her to discuss her incestuous relationship. Her confession seemingly alleviated her own feelings of guilt and somehow enabled her husband to feel more confident, and there were no further episodes of impotence.

Mrs. Bentley's school records, the test results, and the examiner's impressions combine to indicate that her intellectual ability is at least within the average range. On the Wechsler Adult Intelligence Scale she obtained a Verbal IQ of 106, a Performance IQ of 98, and a Full Scale IQ of 103. There were no significant weaknesses save that her ability to immediately recall newly learned material was poor. Her highest successes were in verbal reasoning and in generalized social knowledge. In several minor instances there were substitutions of sounds in several words. It was noted that in responding to many questions she stated that she felt she was doing poorly and that at times she would attempt to cover this feeling by brief bursts of inappropriate laughter. It did not appear that her confidence was increased in situations where she was having obvious successes, and she did not appear to respond to praise.

The personality tests that were administered suggest that Mrs. Bentley has extreme hostility to authority. She has an extremely low self-concept, lack of self-confidence, and apparently believes that she is doomed to failure. She appears to have pervasive, deep feelings of anger which are triggered inappropriately at almost any time. She did not appear to be depressed or to suffer any psychosis. The most significant finding is this woman's complete lack of guilt over the death of her son. She does not appear to see this as being anything unusual or out of the ordinary, and apparently to her it was "just one of those things."

Both Dr. Deady and Dr. Hartner testified at Mrs. Bentley's trial and repeated their opinions that she was not insane, that she could distinguish right from wrong. However, the defense psychiatrist, Dr. Voltman, maintained that Roy's murder was the result of a period of temporary insanity. The judge found her not guilty and ordered her incarcerated at the Lake Shore State Mental Hospital until such a time as her emotional condition permitted her to return home.

The Lake Shore Hospital had a patient population of 3,600 with only 31 physicians on the staff. The administrator was a certified psychiatrist, but the other physicians were self-taught in the area of psychiatry and in the main were men who had failed in other areas of medical specialization. There were three psychologists, one of whom had a Ph.D.; the others had master's degrees. Their contact with patients was limited to testing and evaluation. There were eight social workers, two of whom had professional degrees in social work; the other six did not. Typically a new patient was interviewed by a physician upon admis-

sion. If it was thought necessary, medication was prescribed. The patient's subsequent behavior in the ward was
described by the attendants to the physicians, and a decision to discharge or continue holding the patient depended
largely on the attendants' observation and judgment.
Group therapy was provided once a week. Frequently the
interview on admission was the only contact the patient
had with the physician in charge of his "treatment."

Mrs. Bentley felt quite euphoric when she arrived at the
hospital. She had been found not guilty and was certain
she would not be kept at the hospital long and that she
would soon return to her home and her husband. Once
she was admitted and locked in a ward, however, she became discouraged and depressed.

Margaret Bentley was not given the normal treatment
at the hospital. The publicity of her trial and her subsequent commitment to the hospital had alerted the staff to
the possibility that their treatment of this woman would
be subject to public scrutiny. Therefore she was seen
every day by the admitting physician, and numerous psychological tests were administered.

During her first two weeks at the hospital Margaret
tended to be tense and nervous and somewhat depressed.
But the medication she received appeared to enable her
to relax, and her depression gradually lifted. Talking about
her situation in her sessions with the physician also
seemed to give her considerable relief. Her behavior in the
ward was excellent. She was pleasant, cooperative, and
appeared interested in the problems of other patients. Surprisingly she was well received by the other patients
despite the fact that she had killed her child. The attendants reported that she did not present any management
difficulties, and her days passed pleasantly enough. While
in the hospital it was discovered that she was pregnant.
She was discharged from the Lake Shore Hospital on

January 16, 1970. The discharge summary stated: "At the time of discharge screening she appeared mildly tense and anxious and at times seemed to laugh in a somewhat hysterical manner, but otherwise was able to speak coherently and there was no overt evidence of depression or psychosis. She is to be considered mentally competent and capable of driving. It was pointed out to the patient that if she met strong resistance from relatives or friends regarding the custody of her child, it might be better to permit her child to remain in foster care or in the care of relatives. However, she did not think this was necessary. *Final Diagnosis:* Adult situational reaction with anxiety and depression."

A copy of the discharge summary was sent to the district attorney, whose office leaked the information to local newspapers. There was an immediate burst of publicity with headlines such as: CHILD MURDERER FREED and MOTHER RELEASED AFTER CHILD MURDER.

Dr. George Evison, M.D., the superintendent of Lake Shore Hospital, was irritated to discover that Mrs. Bentley had been released and disgusted with the attending physician's diagnosis. He prepared a statement to appear in the hospital file, with a copy to the district attorney:

> An editorial in the January 24, 1970 edition of the "Daily Herald News" made mention that a Mrs. Margaret Bentley had been sent to Lake Shore State Mental Hospital for treatment. The story went on to say that the staff judged her safe to release, and it was implied that there was no risk or danger to the remaining child from its mother. I was quite surprised to read this as I had no awareness that the patient had ever been at Lake Shore Hospital.
>
> As one sums up the observation and behavior here at this hospital, I would feel that a basic diagnosis of passive-aggressive personality should have been made and would have been an adequate diagnosis with a superimposed reactive depression to the situational problem being present—that is, the killing of her child. I would disagree with the conclusions

and diagnosis of the treating physician where he stated that on the basis of her behavior here at the hospital she would present no apparent danger to the remaining child. This woman's greatest problem was lack of appropriate control under stress, and one gets the feeling that her tolerance is quite limited in dealing with her children and in being able to cope with their activities. The treatment or alteration of a passive-aggressive personality, such as Mrs. Bentley is diagnosed, and the development of more appropriate emotional controls are rarely, if ever, achieved by the amount of psychiatric care received by this woman. I would go a step further and hazard to guess that the modification of a passive-aggressive personality is most unlikely as personality disorders are most resistant to change. I would feel that she remains basically unchanged as compared to the time she committed the act. I do not mean to imply that she is *necessarily* going to harm the remaining child, but I am convinced that her self-control can reach the breaking point with minor stress, and under such circumstances it would be possible that further dangerous acting out might occur.

It should be understood that the court never requested a final report, and it should be made clear that a copy of the ward physician's discharge summary does not represent the official position of this hospital.

Copies of the report were forwarded to the district attorney and to the Juvenile Court. As a result, a further evaluation of Mr. and Mrs. Bentley was ordered made prior to returning Gale to their custody. The examination was made by Dr. Douglas of the County Mental Health Out-Patient Clinic.

COUNTY DEPARTMENT OF PUBLIC HEALTH
MENTAL HEALTH OUT-PATIENT CLINIC
(963) 432-1122   763 Fourth Ave. N.W.

Robert Grednoe, M.D., Director

September 22, 1970

Mr. Regis Stuart
Chief Clerk
Juvenile Division
State Circuit Court

Dear Mr. Stuart:

At the request of the District Attorney's office John and Margaret Bentley were interviewed and given a battery of psychological tests on September 17, 1970. At that time Mrs. Bentley was appropriately dressed, and her initial attitude appeared to be overly conscientious and overly cooperative. She was properly oriented as to time, place, and person, and her stream of thought followed a reasonable progression. There was no evidence of any psychotic ideation or behavior.

As the interview progressed she began to manifest obvious physiological signs of anxiety, becoming extremely restless, continually wringing her hands, tapping the desk, or manipulating the ashtray. Her forehead perspired copiously, and her attitude became increasingly evasive and defensive. Her affect and mood became inappropriate; she laughed and giggled when confronted with difficult or embarrassing questions; and she exhibited no remorse or depression when such reactions would be appropriate. For example, in describing the death of her son, Roy, she described the event in a flat, emotionless voice, and attributed her behavior to the fact that she believed she was anemic and needed iron pills. In response to further questioning about this incident, Mrs. Bentley cited many extenuating circumstances including the fact that she drank too much coffee and that Roy was an extremely irritating child.

This woman's social history indicated that her childhood environment was extremely poor. Her mother was rejecting and unloving. In contrast, her father turned to Margaret after he had been rejected by his wife, and he and Margaret enjoyed a mutually gratifying incestuous relationship for a period of six years. She stated that she was very jealous of her younger brother and that it still irritates her whenever she hears a child cry, inasmuch as it reminds her of the brother that she envied and hated. She is still preoccupied with feelings of rejection by her mother and still engaged in a struggle to win her mother's love and affection.

The results of the intelligence tests which were administered to Mrs. Bentley are consistent with previous findings and indicate that her level of intellectual functioning is in the normal range (IQ 109). Further testing suggests that there there is no impairment of intellectual functioning that might be attributed to cerebral injury or disease.

Mrs. Bentley has been given several psychiatric and psychological evaluations and she has become rather sophisticated in discerning possible implications that might be attached to her responses. In answering the various items on the Minnesota Multiphasic Personality Inventory she consistently made sophisticated attempts to dissimulate and produced a "saw-tooth" profile that was of no diagnostic value except to indicate that she was being highly defensive and evasive. The projective techniques used strongly indicated that Mrs. Bentley has severe unresolved oedipal conflicts; that she is obsessed with feelings of worthlessness and guilt; and that on occasion she has some difficulty in distinguishing between fantasy and reality; that she attempts to control her emotions by rigid, constrictive denial of her feelings, but these attempts fail and upon very slight provocation she becomes extremely angry and irritable and resorts to maladaptive, uncontrolled aggressive behavior.

When Mr. Bentley was interviewed, he was irritated that he should be required to come to this agency, and he expressed some concern about his salary loss. He appeared anxious to appear dominant and controlling in the interview and scoffed at the notion of any psychological evaluation being made of him because of his sophistication which he acquired while taking an elementary course in psychology at the University of Chicago. He appeared free of any overt evidence of psychosis, but he exhibited a high level of neurotic anxiety, particularly as he attempted to find acceptable excuses for his wife's behavior. He admitted some difficulties in their sexual relationship and further admitted that he was often impotent. However, he created the impression that he and his wife were quite accepting of each other and that any problems that they might have in their relationship might be solved by their working together.

A brief battery of psychological tests was administered, and the results suggested that Mr. Bentley's intelligence falls into the bright normal range (IQ 116), and like Mrs. Bentley, there was no evidence to suggest that he was suffering from any organic disorder. It did appear that Mr. Bentley has a basic distrust of others and tends to blame many of his misfortunes and difficulties upon members of his own family and upon persons in authority in the community. His high level of anxiety tends to make him react to minor matters as if they were major emergencies, and in all probability he responds inappropriately to any stressful situation.

It would appear that in this case an anxious, impulsive, aggressive woman with a long history of maladaptive behavior, including incest and physical assault, is married to a man who is suffering from an anxiety neurosis. It would be my opinion that any court or agency that permitted this couple to retain custody of a child was taking a rather dangerous, calculated risk that the child would suffer extreme physical abuse. If this did not occur and the child were not actually subjected to physical harm, it is very difficult for me to conceive that children raised by this couple would not be subjected to environmental pressures that would result in serious psychological damage. I would strongly recommend that the child remain in a foster home and not be returned to this couple.

Very truly yours,
/S/ Samuel Douglas, Ph.D.
Senior Staff Psychologist

Mr. and Mrs. Bentley retained an attorney who advised them of the contents of Dr. Douglas' report. They took no action until after the birth of their third child and then petitioned the court to have Gale returned to their home. The hearing was held on October 5, 1970, with Judge Chester Beshaw presiding. Mr. Fred Perrins represented the parents; the deputy district attorney was Jerry Rusk; and Dr. Douglas and several members of the Bentley family were present as witnesses.

STATE CIRCUIT COURT
Juvenile Division

| In the Matter of |) | No. *87,643* |
| *Gale Bentley, age 5* |) | DISPOSITION AND ORDER |

The above entitled matter having been heard on the *5th* day of *October 1970,* upon the petition of *John and Margaret Bentley* praying that an investigation be made of the circumstances concerning the above named minor, the following persons being present at the hearing: *John and Margaret Bentley, parents; Gale Bentley, minor; Deputy District Attorney Jerry Rusk; Attorney Fred Perrins; witnesses.*

and it appearing to the Court, and the Court finding that:

1. Due notice of this proceeding has been given all persons interested herein.

2. The minor is a citizen of this county and under the jurisdiction of the Court.

The Court being fully advised in the premises:

NOW THEREFORE IT IS HEREBY ADJUDGED
AND ORDERED:

1. The evidence presented here has been largely speculative in nature and evidence has been offered to indicate that Gale Bentley has been subjected to abuse or neglect.

2. Gale Bentley will be made a ward of this court and will be returned to her parents' custody.

3. This arrangement will be supervised by the Welfare Department.

4. The parents are directed to continue psychiatric treatment for a period of at least one year.

Dated this *6th* day of *October 1970.*

/S/ *Chester Beshaw*
_____
                                  Judge

Following this ruling John and Margaret Bentley applied for psychological service at the County Mental Health Out-Patient Clinic. They dutifully appeared for every scheduled appointment, but their attitudes were recalcitrant, and they did not participate in any meaningful discussions with their therapists. Mrs. Bentley was capable of sitting the entire hour without making any comments except trivia about her automobile, her home, or her relatives' activities. She frequently commented that she felt no need for therapy, that everything was all right between her and her husband, and that she was wasting the therapist's time.

In contrast, Mr. Bentley was frequently angry and agitated during the therapy sessions, but his anger was directed at the court rather than at his wife; he, too, frequently stated that therapy was a waste of his time.

After three months a conference was held, at which the Bentleys reiterated their objections to continuing in therapy. As a result, the case was closed. The Welfare Department, which had jurisdiction over Gale, was notified that the therapy had been terminated. They expressed great concern and requested that the director of the clinic reconsider his agency's action.

COUNTY DEPARTMENT OF PUBLIC HEALTH
MENTAL HEALTH OUT-PATIENT CLINIC
(963) 432-1122   763 Fourth Ave. N.W.

Robert Grednoe, M.D., Director

February 23, 1971

Mr. Robert Paley, A.C.S.W.
Director, Children's Division
County Department of Public Welfare

Dear Mr. Paley:
    As agreed in my telephone conversation with Mr. Lawrence, I reviewed the information and evaluations that we have in our file on Mr. and Mrs. John Bentley. I also had an opportunity to discuss Dr. Douglas's report with him and to discuss the case with Drs. Elgin and Koch who had been seeing Mr. and Mrs. Bentley. Both Dr. Elgin and Dr. Koch came to the same conclusion; that is, this couple was not really interested in continuing psychotherapeutic involvement. They felt that they could handle whatever problems they had quite adequately without a third party's intervention. It has been our experience that patients with this kind of attitude and motivation do not profit from further psychotherapy, and in fact, forcing them to continue may well have an adverse effect on the family's interpersonal relationships. Therefore, we feel that we would not wish to pursue any further contact with this couple.
    This does present a problem, I know, with your agency's

involvement with these parents. The court order dated October 5, 1970, reads that "The parents are directed to continue psychiatric treatment for a period of at least one year." I would presume that the intent of this part of the court order was to help the parents gain insight and make positive behavioral changes which then would be a safeguard, preventing incidents of physical abuse to the remaining children in the home. Unfortunately, our evaluations indicate that this safeguard is not possible. For further opinions and recommendations from our agency's contacts with Mr. and Mrs. Bentley I would refer to Dr. Douglas' report of September 22, 1970, which should be in your files.

I can only suggest at this time that perhaps the next course of action to be taken is to review the case with Judge Beshaw and then decide what further action, if any, can be taken to safeguard the children from physical harm and emotional deprivation. If you feel that further discussion with our staff about this situation would prove useful, please do not hesitate to contact us again.

Very truly yours,

/S/ Robert Grednoe, M.D.
Director

On May 3, 1971, Mr. and Mrs. Bentley took Gale to a physician. They reported to him that she had fallen and were afraid that she had broken her arm. The examination revealed that the child's arm was indeed broken, but the physician noted that three fingernails had been torn off one of her hands. He notified the police.

DEPARTMENT OF PUBLIC SAFETY
BUREAU OF POLICE
Officer's Report

1. Specific Crime	2. Place of Occurrence	3. Case No.
Assault – Child abuse	Undetermined	72-2010

4. Date and Time Crime Occurred Undetermined date prior to 5/2/71	5. Date and Time Crime Reported 5/3/71 3:15 PM
6. Victim's Name Gale Bentley	7. Person Reporting Crime Charles Renton, MD
8. Witnesses' Names Charles Renton, MD 6080 Raleigh Bldg.	9. Suspect(s) Name John Bentley, father Margaret Bentley, mother

10. Narrative of Crime, Describe Evidence, Summarize Details Not Given Above.

At about 3:20 PM, 5/2/71 received 219 from Radio Div. and proceeded to 6080 Raleigh Bldg. Interviewed complainant Dr. Charles Renton who reported that victim was brought to his office by John and Margaret Bentley, the parents. Dr. Renton said victim suffered fractured right arm and three fingernails torn off left hand. Said injuries occurred while victim was in custody of parents, and that it was unlikely that injuries could have been accidents.

Interviewed John and Margaret Bentley and advised them of their rights. They refused to talk except in presence of attorney. Placed this couple under arrest and escorted them to station.

/S/ Robert Kelly
Badge No. 4111
Day Relief

Both children were removed to the Wilson Shelter for Children. While in the Shelter, Gale was found to be very withdrawn, uncommunicative, and unresponsive. The parents visited her regularly, but the visitations appeared unsatisfactory. Gale was not upset to see her parents either come or go. During the visits Mr. Bentley would sit on the couch staring straight ahead for the entire hour and not communicate in any way with his daughter. Mrs. Bentley did somewhat better, usually holding Gale on her lap and sometimes reading stories to her. Mary Jane, the younger child, would sit rigidly on her mother's lap, staring straight ahead with no display of warmth or affection. Prior to the Juvenile Court hearing both Mr. and Mrs. Bentley were again referred to the County Mental Health Out-Patient Clinic for another evaluation.

COUNTY DEPARTMENT OF PUBLIC HEALTH
MENTAL HEALTH OUT-PATIENT CLINIC
(963) 432-1122   763 Fourth Ave. N.W.

Robert Grednoe, M.D., Director

June 15, 1971

Mr. Regis Stuart
Chief Clerk
Juvenile Division
State Circuit Court

Dear Mr. Stuart:

As you know, Mrs. Bentley has been once again referred to this agency for an evaluation. Inasmuch as our previous findings and recommendations were largely ignored by the court, it is difficult to perceive the value of further evaluation. You will recall that Dr. Douglas wrote in part: "It would be my opinion that any court or agency that permitted this couple to retain custody of a child was taking a rather dangerous, calculated risk that the child would suffer extreme physical abuse. If this did not occur and the child were not actually subjected to physical harm, it is very difficult for me to conceive that children raised by this couple would not be subjected to environmental pressures that would result in serious psychological damage."

It now appears that Dr. Douglas' fears were justified and that further injury to the Bentley children has occurred, in that the little girl has a broken arm and the fingernails torn from one hand. It would appear to me that the record of child abuse by this couple would be sufficient evidence for your court, or any sane body, to make a determination that Mr. and Mrs. Bentley were unfit parents. A repetition of our previous evaluations would serve no useful purpose.

Very truly yours,

/S/ Robert Grednoe, M.D.
Director

Prior to the hearing Deputy District Attorney Rusk held a long conference with Gale. The child freely told him that her mother had torn off her fingernails as punishment for feeding a stray cat that had appeared at the Bentley home. She said that she was crying afterwards and that her mother jerked her arm to make her be quiet and that at that time she thought that her arm was broken. However, she told Mr. Rusk that she would not ever tell these things in front of her mother and father because they would punish her severely for it.

Because there was no evidence that could be presented that would show how and by whom the crime against Gale had been committed, criminal prosecution was abandoned, and a dependency petition was submitted. The hearing was held on July 5, 1971, with Judge Beshaw presiding. Attorney Fred Perrins represented the parents, and Deputy District Attorney Jerry Rusk represented the state. Dr. Douglas was asked to testify once again, as were relatives of the parents and numerous witnesses from social agencies.

Judge Beshaw refused to permit Gale to testify privately and insisted that if she were to be called on, her testimony must be given in the presence of her parents, and that she must be subjected to examination by the parents' attorney. Under these circumstances Mr. Rusk believed that he would be ill-advised to call for the girl's testimony. The testimony of the other witnesses followed the pattern established at previous hearings. Dr. Douglas testified as to the parents' lack of emotional stability, and the relatives testified that Mr. and Mrs. Bentley were adequate parents. The judicial decision was rendered on July 6, 1971.

Juvenile Division
STATE CIRCUIT COURT

In the Matter of	)	*No. 87,939*
Gale Bentley, age 6	)	DISPOSITION AND ORDER
Mary Jane Bentley, age	)	
10 months	)	

The above entitled matter having been heard on the *6th* day of *July 1971,* upon the petition of *the District Attorney* praying that an investigation be made of the circumstances concerning the above named minor, the following persons being present at the hearing: *John and Margaret Bentley, parents; Gale Bentley, minor; Mary Jane Bentley, minor; Deputy District Attorney Jerry Rusk; Attorney Fred Perrins; witnesses.*

and it appearing to the Court, and the Court finding that:
1. Due notice of this proceeding has been given all persons interested herein.
2. The minor is a citizen of this county and under the jurisdiction of the Court.
The Court being fully advised in the premises:

NOW THEREFORE IT IS HEREBY ADJUDGED
AND ORDERED:

   1. The evidence presented suggests that Gale Bentley suffered serious harm while in the custody of her parents.
   2. Wardship is maintained and Gale and Mary Jane Bentley will be returned to parental custody.
   3. Parents are admonished to be exceedingly careful to prevent further injury to these children.
   4. Department of Welfare will exercise supervision.

Dated this 7*th* day of *July 1971.*

/S/ *Chester Beshaw*
_____
Judge

The children are now living with their parents. The only supervision is provided by a welfare worker who stops briefly at the Bentley home on the second Monday of each month. The Benteys are well prepared for her visit and make sure that the children are neat and clean and that the house is in perfect order. They are desperately anxious not to receive an adverse report.

Every professional person who has been involved in this case is positive that future harm will occur to these children who have been deserted by the state. However, they are powerless to act and can only wait until these children are punished once again in some vicious, inhumane way.

Chapter 10   HENRY

> This young man has been given three valid, widely accepted IQ tests on three recent occasions by three different certified psychologists at our agency. They agree that his present level of intellectual functioning is in the bright normal range despite his long period of incarceration in a school for the mentally retarded.
>
> —*A psychiatrist's testimony*

Henry Fromm's life started badly. His mother's labor was long and difficult, and at the time of delivery there was a breech presentation which necessitated turning the child in the womb prior to birth. During this process pressure was brought to bear upon the cord leading from the placenta to the fetus, and the brain was deprived of oxygen for several minutes. This caused irreversible brain damage in some of the motor and sensory areas and resulted in cerebral palsy.

Henry's parents, George and Doris Fromm, were both overachievers who set high goals for themselves. They had been raised in a small farming community in North Dakota and very early in life had both determined to make every effort to escape from that environment. They were both fine students, maintaining nearly perfect A averages from the first grade through college. They were married shortly after graduation and moved to the city where George entered law school and Doris found a job with an advertising agency. After completing his legal training George became a successful lawyer.

The Fromms wanted nothing but the best. Before making any purchase they consulted consumer publications and made every effort to ensure that their cars and every appliance and piece of furniture that went into their home were of excellent quality.

They had eagerly looked forward to Henry's birth. In view of their achievements thus far, they expected to have a child who would emulate them and who would also be a high-achieving, "perfect" child. Henry was a catastrophic disappointment.

During the early months of Henry's life his parents believed him to be a healthy, normal child and showered him with affection. They noted, however, that he seemed to have difficulty keeping his mouth closed. It was almost as if his tongue were too large for his mouth, and he salivated continuously. The movements of his hands and legs were not smooth; it seemed as if he jerked them from one position to another. Their pediatrician confirmed their fears and advised them that their son had serious neurological problems.

As Henry developed he was very slow in acquiring the ability to crawl, and it was impossible for him to stand and walk alone. His speech was extremely slow and halting, with frequent stutters and strange sounds. It was very difficult for George and Doris to be proud of Henry. He was a grotesque caricature of a normal child. His struggles to move and speak gradually became an unbearable irritant to them.

All the Fromms' friends had healthy, happy, normal babies. It seemed to George and Doris that their friends were patronizing them. Somehow Henry's disabilities seemed to be the fault of his parents, an area of endeavor in which they had failed. Henry's agonizing efforts to move and play pervaded the couple with a sense of shame.

Their pediatrician attempted to assure them that Henry was not totally incapacitated, that he seemed to be of normal intelligence and that it might be possible for him to have a reasonably happy, successful life despite his severe handicaps. But it was difficult for George and Doris to believe this, since their child, whom they were coming to see as a sort of monster, seemed incapable fo performing the simplest tasks.

During the early years of President Kennedy's administration the Fromms were solicited for funds for the Kennedy Schools for Exceptional Children. They became more aware of the problem of mental retardation and learned that many parents placed their children in suitable training facilities, where, hopefully, the children could be trained and educated to their full potential. The notion that Henry belonged in such a school was an attractive one; it provided an escape from an impossible situation which would be helpful to the boy and at the same time ease their consciences. Doris had recently given birth to a baby daughter who was a completely normal child, so they were particularly eager to have Henry out of the house.

Their search revealed that the only possible training school in their state in which Henry could be placed was the Green River Training School, an institution for the mentally retarded operated by the state mental health department. Its buildings were antiquated; its programs were inadequate; and its staff was poorly trained and too small to bring about any positive changes in most of the students there. In short, it was a dumping ground for unwanted children. But the Fromms decided to go ahead and place Henry there.

In order to have a child admitted to the Green River School it was necessary that a physician certify that the child was mentally retarded. George and Doris asked their pediatrician to prepare the certificate. They were somewhat taken aback when he refused to do so, stating that in his opinion Henry was probably of at least average intelligence, but that his speech problems made it difficult to ascertain his true intellectual level. After some discussion the pediatrician reluctantly agreed to have Henry evaluated by a psychologist in an effort to determine the boy's level of intellectual functioning.

The psychologist's report was quite guarded; it pointed out the difficulty of evaluating a boy of Henry's age with his level of speech and motor impairment. Virtually every intelligence test had performance tasks and verbal tasks, and Henry's disabilities made such tests extremely difficult for him. The psychologist did express the opinion that Henry was of at least normal intelligence and certainly not retarded. He strongly advised against placement in the Green River School. After reviewing the psychologist's findings the pediatrician refused to consider Henry mentally retarded and advised the Fromms he would not certify him for admission to the school.

George and Doris were disgruntled. They believed that they had been victimized, first by the fate that had given them a child with cerebral palsy and second by an obstinate physician who refused to concede the obvious, that Henry suffered from serious mental retardation and should be hospitalized.

Henry bothered his father more and more. Meals were a particularly difficult time; since Henry had difficulty lifting a fork to his mouth, he slobbered continuously, and often bits of food would drop from his mouth as he attempted to chew. He knew that this displeased his father and would attempt to say he was sorry, but speech was so difficult and Henry was so poorly coordinated that he would sometimes attempt to apologize while he was chewing and spew food onto the table. Little by little George abandoned his attempts at self-control and would slap Henry unmercifully for any behavior or accident that George found embarrassing. They never permitted Henry to be present when there were guests in the home, and as months passed they

became more and more convinced that the boy was retarded and should be in Green River School. It would be
such an easy out.

In despair George and Doris consulted with several other
physicians and finally located Dr. Cleve Bennett who was
sympathetic to their view. He examined Henry briefly and
confirmed the diagnosis of cerebral palsy. He pointed out
that in 50 or 60 percent of the cases of C.P., some degree
of mental retardation is present. As a result of his examination he agreed that Henry was retarded. He signed the necessary papers and after a brief waiting period Henry was
admitted to the Green River Training School.

Henry was almost six years old when he was admitted to
the school. When his parents delivered him, he was taken
by an attendant who helped him to a receiving unit where
his clothes and a few personal belongings were taken and
he was scrubbed and issued school uniforms. He was then
taken to the ward that would be his home for the next
ten years.

Many of the other children in the ward were little more
than vegetables, barely able to dress and feed themselves,
and who were content to spend extended periods of time
completely idle. Other children who approached normal intelligence were loud and boisterous. They frequently teased
Henry, tripping him as he attempted to walk and mimick-
ing his halting, defective speech. Older retarded boys in the
ward were kinder, and several of them would help Henry
move about the ward and get him to the dining room. The
food was sparse and of poor quality. Because the school
was overcrowded, the children were served in shifts. This
required them to eat rapidly, and Henry was frequently
hustled from his table before he was able to eat a complete meal.

Several of the attendants were sorry for the boy and

made sporadic attempts to entertain him or to provide him with some companionship, but their workloads were so heavy that they could spend little time with him.

Six months after Henry was admitted to the school, he was placed in formal academic classes and learned to read. Despite his many handicaps, he learned to read quickly and well, astonishing his teachers. They frequently commented to the physicians in charge that Henry did not appear to be retarded. The only response the physicians made to their inquiries were comments such as "some of them will fool you," and it was pointed out that many of the boys developed well in certain specific areas such as reading or arithmetic, but that their overall level of intelligence was within the retarded range.

With the passage of years Henry depended more and more on books to provide him an escape from the environment in which he had been placed. He read for amusement and often would read to acquire new knowledge. He progressed rapidly in the areas of arithmetic, science, and social sciences, and the level of his work was usually comparable to that of a normal child.

His parents faithfully visited him once a month and spent an hour with him. His language handicap was so great that he had difficulty communicating with them. His father's contempt for him was obvious and effectively discouraged the boy from attempting to describe his scholastic achievements. Routine reports from the school to the parents merely described his progress as being satisfactory.

Several fraternal organizations provided volunteer workers who spent some time with the children in the school. They would visit at least once every two weeks and bring suitable presents for the children who had been assigned to them. They would also take them on frequent outings. Eventually Henry was assigned to such a worker, a middle-aged woman who had raised her own children and who was deeply interested in children with special problems. She was extremely kind and patient and sat quietly while Henry stammered in his attempts to talk. It eventually became obvious to her that his choice of words and the topics he discussed were not compatible with the notion that he was a retarded child. She arranged for them to visit the Museum of Science, where Henry displayed a keen interest in the exhibits and quite obviously understood some of the more difficult scientific principles that were illustrated. His volunteer worker was most impressed and determined that Henry had been victimized by being placed in the Green River School.

It was difficult for her to get the school authorities to act. She besieged the superintendent and found him a peculiarly evasive man who seemed determined to avoid having a competent psychologist or a child psychiatrist evaluate Henry. Finally, in disgust and despair, the worker hired a psychologist who was in private practice to come to the Green River School and make an evaluation of the boy. The psychologist found that Henry's level of intellectual functioning was in the superior range, and while he obviously had many impaired abilities, he was not mentally retarded and should not be permitted to remain in the institution.

The psychologist's report was taken to the superintendent who finally agreed to have the school's own psychologist evaluate Henry. The results were the same. He was a boy of superior intelligence.

After receiving the psychologist's report, the superintendent of the school advised Mr. and Mrs. Fromm that their son was no longer considered mentally retarded and therefore that placement in the school was inappropriate. He advised them that Henry would be discharged and asked them to come and pick him up at their earliest opportunity. George and Doris were appalled. They now had three children, all of whom were happy and normal. They could not tolerate having Henry, their monster, back at home. They appeased their consciences by telling one another that the school was in error, that Henry *was* mentally retarded.

After some discussion Mr. Fromm engaged one of his colleagues as an attorney and secured an injunction from a court prohibiting the Green River School from discharging Henry. The judge, in granting the injunction, stipulated that another independent evaluation of Henry's intellectual capacity should be made. As a result, Henry was referred to the County Mental Health Out-Patient Clinic.

The chief psychologist at the clinic found it incredible that Henry could have been retained in the Green River Training School for so many years unless he was actually mentally retarded. But he assigned a staff psychologist to evaluate the boy. This was done, and the psychologist reported that Henry's IQ was approximately 142. The chief psychologist was astonished and requested a second psychologist to make another evaluation. Using a different intelligence test this psychologist obtained an IQ of 138. The chief psychologist was again astonished at these findings, which to him indicated years of appalling waste in Henry's life, conducted a third evaluation and obtained an IQ of 140.

These findings were reported to the court when a second hearing was held and as a result, the injunction was lifted and the Green River School discharged Henry.

Henry's return home was a failure. His father could not tolerate him. Whenever the boy had difficulty eating, his father swore at him or cuffed him about the head. At last Mrs. Fromm realized that the situation could not continue. Through the Welfare Department, arrangements were made to place Henry in a foster home.

Foster parents were found who were sympathetic and interested, and Henry was made to feel loved and welcome. He is presently enrolled in a regular high school, has kept a straight A average, and plans to go to college and eventually to medical school. There is every reason to believe that he will succeed.

Chapter 11   HOWARD SPANGLER

The wife was at work, and I was watching the kids—Joanna, the six-month-old, and Larry, the two-year-old. I went out to the kitchen to get a cup of coffee, and when I came back, Joanna was just lying on the floor, quiet, with her eyes open. She didn't move, so after a while I phoned my wife, and we took her to the hospital. The doctor said her skull was fractured. I guess the other kid must have done it while I was in the kitchen.

—*A father's statement*

Howard Spangler was unlucky. Through most of his life it appeared that he had been an innocent bystander when crimes or antisocial activities occurred, yet somehow he had been implicated and punished. For example, when Howard was 10 years old, he was found in an empty school building on Saturday morning. The door to the principal's office had been forced open, and the petty cash and stamps had been stolen. These were found in Howard's pocket. He explained that it really wasn't his fault at all. He had been playing in the school yard and noticed that one of the school doors was open. He was curious and a little worried, he said, so he entered the school building and was confronted by the boy who had stolen the cash and stamps. Howard explained to him that it was wrong to steal, so the boy gave them to Howard to replace. Howard was on his way to the principal's office to put the stamps and money back when the police appeared. He was offended when the police refused to believe his story. At his hearing at the Juvenile Court he adopted the role of the indignant innocent. Nevertheless, he was sentenced to house arrest for six months, which meant that his parents were responsible for watching him at all times.

161

During the following year the school caught fire, and Howard was seen running from the building. He was arrested, and explained to the police that he had just been walking by and thought he smelled smoke. He said that he went to the front door of the building to investigate, and when he saw the flames, he started to run to call the fire department. Subsequent investigation revealed that some highly combustible material, probably gasoline, had been spread throughout the school before the fire was set. It was learned that Howard had purchased gasoline in a container from a neighborhood service station an hour before the fire occurred. When confronted with this circumstantial evidence, Howard explained that he had bought the gasoline to give to an older friend who owned a boat and needed it for the outboard motor. When pressed, Howard could not remember the name of the friend. As a result of this incident, Howard was sentenced to a six-month term in the Boys' Industrial School.

Three months after he was discharged from the school, he was apprehended leaving a store with a transistor radio that he had not paid for. He was arrested and charged with shoplifting. Again he had an explanation: another, unnamed, friend had told him that he had to go downtown and had asked Howard to hold the radio for him. This episode sent Howard back to the Boys' Industrial School for another six months.

Howard was 15 when he was arrested while driving his first stolen car. He admitted that he had taken the car, but denied that he meant to steal it. He claimed that he just meant to drive around the block two or three times to "see how it feels." While awaiting a hearing on this charge, he was apprehended driving a second stolen car. This time Howard maintained that a friend had loaned the car to him and that he did not know the car was stolen. These two events resulted in Howard being sentenced to the Boys' Industrial School for a period not to exceed two years.

During this stay at the school it was noted that Howard was becoming violent and aggressive. As he matured he became a powerful young man who often attacked other inmates with little or no provocation. Whenever disciplinary hearings about these attacks were held, Howard steadfastly maintained that he was the one who had been provoked; never did he admit to any guilt or remorse.

After Howard had served his sentence he was released and returned to his parents' home. Three weeks later a bank was robbed. The police were nearby and followed the getaway car. After a chase of several miles the robbers were apprehended and it was discovered that Howard had been driving the car. He had a small calibre revolver tucked under his shirt. Once again Howard denied his guilt. He stated that he just happened to be sitting in the car in front of the bank with the motor running when the bandits emerged and forced him to drive them away. He explained that as capture became inevitable, one of the bandits "hid" the revolver under his shirt. The jury thought little of this explanation, and Howard was sentenced to a five-year term at the state penitentiary. He was paroled after serving two years of the sentence.

While on parole Howard made sporadic attempts to find a job. He began to drink heavily and was regularly stoned, either on marijuana or alcohol. He was fired from each job soon after he found it and invariably found some reason to blame his employer for the job termination.

His parents had abandoned all efforts to rehabilitate Howard, and he could not depend on them for support. He resorted to numerous petty crimes to get money. He was not apprehended for any of these crimes. He continued to be ill-tempered and frequently got in fights. He was particularly hot tempered when he was drinking. Finally he was arrested while drunk after having a fight with a bartender. His parole was revoked, and he was returned to the state penitentiary to serve the remainder of his sentence.

Howard was 23 years old when he was released from the penitentiary. He had grown into a tall, vigorous man who was rather handsome and who appeared to have a pleasing personality. He found it easy to make new acquaintances, but his behavior was such that it was difficult for him to form lasting friendships.

Shortly after his release Howard found a job in an auto body shop and began to learn the trade. Surprisingly, he did quite well. The owner, a tolerant person, was willing to overlook Howard's occasional periods of intoxication, and his absences did not cause any undue concern. It appeared that at long last Howard had begun to settle down and to avoid criminal activities.

Howard met Marie in the autumn of 1966. She was 20, a vividly beautiful girl with dark black hair and dark blue eyes. She was a gay, vivacious girl who thought Howard was charming and who was excited by his virile masculinity. They were married five weeks later.

Marie had an excellent job as a secretary. She enjoyed her work and frequently volunteered to work overtime or to help out on special jobs that arose from time to time. As a result she was highly valued by her employer, and her salary was higher than that of the average secretary. Within a month after their marriage Howard announced that he was tired of working in the body shop and quit. He pointed out that they could easily live on Marie's salary until he found a job that was suited to his particular life style and aspirations.

During the next year Howard lived what was for him an exceedingly good life. He seldom got up before noon. After a hurried breakfast he went to a tavern where he spent the day drinking and playing pool. He was seldom home before 8 or 9 in the evening, and he never offered to help Marie with household tasks or the cooking. Whenever she managed to find the courage to protest, he beat her severely. Within a few months she was too terrified to express her concerns.

Howard's life style was threatened when Marie became pregnant. He realized at once that she would have to quit work after a few months and that would leave them with no resources except meager allotments from welfare or what he could earn himself. He beat Marie again and again and accused her of carelessness in permitting the pregnancy to occur. He tried to persuade her to have an abortion, but she was a faithful Catholic and refused to consider this solution.

Howard still had not found work by the time Marie had to quit her job, so they applied for and received assistance from the Welfare Department. Howard was grossly dissatisfied with the amount of money they received and frequently protested to their social worker that they could not exist on such a small amount. Actually the monetary crisis was much greater than Howard let on, because of his continuing habit of spending his time in neighborhood taverns. Marie frequently had very little to eat and was forced to ask her parents for help. This was given grudgingly because Marie's father was convinced that Howard could easily get a job and should support his wife.

After their son Larry was born, Marie returned to work. This pleased Howard. After a few weeks he began using Marie's earnings to finance an affair with another woman. Marie discovered this and protested. Howard's reply was to beat her once again, and Marie gradually accepted an existence of uncertainty and unhappiness. Her only joys were Larry and her job.

Howard could not tolerate having Larry cry. He would

slap the child unmercifully and the hurt boy would only scream louder. Marie pleaded with him to leave the child alone and hired a babysitter to stay with the boy when she was at work. But the babysitter was sometimes unable to come; after one such day when the child was home alone with Howard, Marie noticed that its eyes were swollen and puffy as if the baby had been punched. She questioned Howard about it, and he exploded, "Yes, Godammit. I hit the squalling little brat, and I'll hit you if you don't shut up about it."

Marie took the child to a physician and was assured that the injuries were only superficial. She explained to the physician that the injuries had occurred because she had accidently dropped the child while preparing his bath. The unsuspecting physician took no action.

Four months later Larry was beaten again, this time much more severely. His nose was broken; his lips were cut; and two of his teeth were broken off. Once again Marie took the child to a physician, a new one unfamiliar with the family, whom she randomly selected from the phone directory. She explained that the injuries had been incurred when she was changing the boy's diaper, and a leaf on the table collapsed dropping him on the edge of a chair and then to the floor. Once again a harried physician saw no cause to doubt Marie's account and no action was taken.

The next time Larry was beaten, Marie told a third physician that it occurred when a cabinet door snapped shut unexpectedly and the child was dropped. Subsequently she told a variety of physicians that the crib had collapsed, that there had been an auto accident, that she had slipped on a wet floor and dropped the baby. None of the several physicians who were asked to treat these injuries suspected that they were inflicted by the father, and none of them saw fit to have the injuries investigated.

When Larry was 18 months old, a second child, Joanna, was born. Marie's pregnancy had been punctuated with violent outbursts by Howard who accused her of trapping him into staying with the marriage because of the children that she was having. He disliked Joanna from the first and never showed her any love or affection. When she was six months old it became necessary for Howard to stay with the children because the babysitter could not come. Joanna was restive in her crib and cried frequently. Howard became angry at the way the child was "bothering" him. He picked her from her crib and threw her across the room.

Howard became alarmed when Joanna remained motionless. He realized that he might be accused of having committed a crime, so he gathered up the limp, motionless child and took her to the Holy Angels Hospital. He had phoned Marie and she met him there. The child was admitted to the hospital, and the resident on duty, Dr. Richard Hummel, questioned Howard as to how the accident occurred. Howard professed ignorance as to what happened and suggested that his son, Larry, who was less than three years old, had inflicted the injuries on the child. Dr. Hummel did not believe his story and called the police.

DEPARTMENT OF PUBLIC SAFETY
BUREAU OF POLICE
Officer's Report

1. Specific Crime	2. Place of Occurrence	3. Case No.
Assault (Child abuse)	61771 Woodford Rd.	70-1680

4. Date and Time Crime Occurred	5. Date and Time Crime Reported
8/17/70 About 10:00 AM	8/17/70 11:40 AM

6. Victim's Name	7. Person Reporting Crime
Joanna Spangler – Age 6 mo.	Richard Hummel, MD Resident, Holy Angels Hospital

8. Witnesses' Names	9. Suspect(s) Name
Marie Spangler (Mother of victim, wife of suspect) 61771 Woodford Rd.	Howard Spangler (Father of Victim) 61771 Woodford Rd.

10. Narrative of Crime, Describe Evidence, Summarize Details Not Given Above.

Received 219 and proceeded to Holy Angels Hospital and made contact with Dr. Richard Hummel who informed writer that victim, Joanna Spangler, had fractured skull and other injuries. Said explanation given by father not satisfactory and that he suspected that this was a case of child abuse.

Both parents were at hospital. Interviewed them and advised them of their rights, and that Writer believed that a crime had been committed. Both agreed to talk and said saw no need to have an attorney present at that time.

Howard Spangler interviewed first, alone. He stated that he did not know how injuries occurred. Said he had been home with the victim, and left her alone in room with two year old brother, Larry, and went to kitchen. When he returned found victim unconscious on floor. Said he guessed two year old Larry must have hit victim on head. Could not explain how this could happen, or why two year old boy would hit victim. Suspect admits that he has been in trouble with police and that he has done time.

Interviewed Marie Spangler alone. She admitted suspect was cruel to children and that she was

11. Continuation of Officer's Report

afraid to leave children with him, but had to
because she worked and supported family. Said had
no actual knowledge of this incident but thought
suspect must have done it.

Warned suspect and wife that they might be needed
for further questioning, and reported to Women's
and Children's Protective Division that there was
another minor child in this home.

/S/ Larry Donahue
Badge No. 6101
Day Relief

Because of Marie's statement to the police, Larry was removed from the home and placed in the Wilson Shelter for
Children. A complete medical examination was made of the
boy. There was radiologic evidence that his arms had been
broken several times and had not set properly. In view of
this a dependency petition was submitted to the court asking that Howard and Marie be declared unfit parents and
asking that Larry and Joanna be made wards of the court
and placed in foster homes. At the preliminary hearing the
referee ordered that a psychiatric or psychological examination be made of both parents. Dr. Samuel Douglas of
the County Mental Health Out-Patient Clinic made an evaluation of both parents. He reported:

COUNTY DEPARTMENT OF PUBLIC HEALTH
MENTAL HEALTH OUT-PATIENT CLINIC
(963) 432-1122   763 Fourth Ave. N.W.

Robert Grednoe, M.D., Director

September 5, 1970

Mr. Regis Stuart
Chief Clerk
Juvenile Division
State Circuit Court

Dear Mr. Stuart:

Mr. and Mrs. Howard Spangler were interviewed and tested on September 1, 1970.

HOWARD SPANGLER: At the time of the interview Mr. Spangler was dressed in a somewhat flashy manner, with a vividly colored bow tie and an iridescent jacket. He wore rings on three fingers of each hand. He appeared very friendly and affable and attempted to turn the interview into a social situation with much inappropriate joking and laughter. He appeared to be free of any overt evidence of anxiety or depression and he did not appear to be suffering from any psychotic ideation.

Several psychological tests were administered. The results would indicate that Mr. Spangler's level of intellectual functioning is in the bright normal range, with an IQ of 114. The tests would further suggest that this man is free of any organic brain dysfunction that might cause impulsive or erratic behavior.

Mr. Spangler's personality appeared to be blatantly antisocial with strong evidence of a fully developed sociopathic personality. It would appear that he tends to be immature, over-active, irresponsible, and impulsive with shallow and superficial interpersonal relationships. This man is basically egocentric, self-centered, and selfish, and demands immediate gratification of all of his impulses and lacks the ability to foresee the consequences of his behavior.

Typically persons such as Mr. Spangler stumble through life from one troubled period to another, destroying whatever close personal relationships others may try to establish with them, and frequently are arrested for poorly planned, ill-conceived crimes.

MARIE SPANGLER: Mrs. Spangler's present level of intellectual functioning is also in the bright normal range with an IQ of 118. Like her husband, there was no evidence of any organic brain damage or dysfunction.

At the time of the interview Mrs. Spangler was quite distraught. While she did not concede that her husband meant to harm the children in any way, she did state that marriage to him was an extremely difficult arrangement and expressed strong feelings of hopelessness. She maintained that she loved him very much and pointed out that when he was in a good mood, he was a very pleasant companion and a most satisfactory lover. She does not want to separate from this man, but she cannot conceive of going on unless changes are made. She readily admitted that she did not believe that her husband would change, but she also stated that she did not feel that her feelings of love and tenderness for him would change either. Therefore, she saw herself in a bind for which there was no solution.

The psychological tests indicated that this woman is not psychotic, but that she is suffering from a moderate depressive neurosis that is the result of the situation in which she finds herself. She is unable to sleep; she is flooded with feelings of inadequacy and guilt, and is rather tense and restless. Her appetite is very poor, and she finds it difficult to "get started" on any new tasks that face her.

DISCUSSION: It would be my opinion that Mr. Spangler's personality is so disordered that he could never function adequately as a father. Marie Spangler's depression would probably dissipate if her situation in life were improved. However, it is unlikely that this will occur, and I would imagine that she will continue to be a depressed individual who has difficulty functioning in any area of life.

In view of the history of child abuse in this family, I would strongly recommend that the children involved be made wards of the court and placed in foster homes.

Very truly yours,
/S/ Samuel Douglas, Ph.D.
Senior Staff Psychologist

The final hearing was scheduled for 10 a.m., November 10, 1970 in Room 240 of the Juvenile Court building. Dr. Douglas accidentally learned at 9:30 that the location of the hearing had been changed to Room 611 of the County Building. He arrived just as the hearing was about to begin and was startled to find that no one was present except the judge, Mr. and Mrs. Spangler, and their attorney, Mr. Peter Rogers. The deputy district attorney and all of the prosecution witnesses were absent. Rather than sitting quietly and permitting the hearing to proceed, Dr. Douglas interrupted the judge to point out that the deputy district attorney and his witnesses were not present and that they probably were not aware that the site of the hearing had been changed.

The judge took the position that it was not his responsibility if the prosecution was not present. Dr. Douglas objected strenuously, was found in contempt of court, and was fined $50.

STATE CIRCUIT COURT
Juvenile Division

| In the Matter of |) | *No. 91,666* |
| *Spangler children* |) DISPOSITION AND ORDER |

The above entitled matter having been heard on the *10th* day of *November 1970,* upon the petition of *Police Department* praying that an investigation be made of the circumstances concerning the above named minors, the following persons being present at the hearing: *Howard and Marie Spangler, parents; Larry and Joanna Spangler, minors; Mr. Peter Rogers, attorney.*

and it appearing to the Court, and the Court finding that:
1. Due notice of this proceeding has been given all persons interested herein.
2. The minor is a citizen of this county and under the jurisdiction of the Court.
The Court being fully advised in the premises:
NOW THEREFORE IT IS HEREBY ADJUDGED AND ORDERED:

1. Mrs. Marie Spangler admitted to harsh treatment of the children in this home.
2. Larry and Joanna Spangler are made wards of this court and returned to their parents' home under the supervision of the Welfare Department.

Dated this *11th* day of *November 1970.*

/S/ *Paul Cermack*
Judge

The following year Howard Spangler was arrested for statutory rape. Because he was released on bail, the Welfare Department, which had responsibility for supervising the children, had them returned to the Wilson Shelter for Children. Physical examinations were made and evidence of additional fractures was found. The children were kept in the Wilson Shelter until Howard's conviction, when they were returned to the custody of their mother.

Both children are extremely inhibited, and it is difficult to persuade either of them to talk. It is obvious that the repeated beatings they have received from their father have resulted in serious, probably irreversible, psychological damage.

Chapter 12 ALICE AND HER FATHER

> Her mother was never close to me; she was always wrapped up in what the neighbors were doing. She didn't seem to care about sex one way or another. As my daughter grew up we became very close and talked together more and more. She got to seem more like a wife than a daughter, so we just started going to bed together.
>
> —*A father's statement*

Leif Nyland was liked and respected in his community. He was employed as an airplane engine mechanic, a trade he had learned while in the air force, from which he had received an honorable discharge. He was a Boy Scout leader, an active church member, and coached a Little League baseball team.

Connie Nyland, Leif's wife, was much less active in community affairs, but was a pleasant, likable person, who was thought of as being a "good neighbor." Their only child, 14-year-old Alice, was liked by everyone. She had an excellent reputation at school and among the members of church groups to which she belonged.

It was difficult for the Harpers, next door neighbors, to believe Alice when she beat on their door one night asking them to protect her, claiming that her father had been abusing her sexually. Not knowing what else to do, they told her to come in the house and telephoned her mother. Mrs. Nyland was angry when she heard what Alice had done and assured the Harpers that Alice's allegations were not true. She explained that Mr. Nyland had refused Alice permission to date several undesirable boys and that Alice was quite angry because of this. She was spreading these terrible stories about her father to get even with him.

Mrs. Nyland went to the Harpers' house and insisted

that Alice come home with her. Alice refused, and broke away from her mother and the Harpers. She ran to the nearest phone booth and called the police.

DEPARTMENT OF PUBLIC SAFETY
BUREAU OF POLICE
Officer's Report

1. Specific Crime	2. Place of Occurrence	3. Case No.
Statutory Rape	4623 Kennedy Ave.	70–1420

4. Date and Time Crime Occurred	5. Date and Time Crime Reported
Over five year period beginning 1965	10:15 PM – 4/12/70

6. Victim's Name	7. Person Reporting Crime
Alice Nyland – Age 14	Victim

8. Witnesses' Names	9. Suspect(s) Name
None	Leif Nyland – father of victim 4623 Kennedy Ave.

10. Narrative of Crime, Describe Evidence, Summarize Details Not Given Above.

Received 219 from Radio Div. app. 10:20 PM, 4/12/70. Proceeded to phone booth at corner of Kennedy Ave. and Ridge Rd. and met victim. Victim stated that she had been repeatedly raped by father, Leif Nyland, over period of about five years. Said didn't want to, but father made her do it. Said father wouldn't let her date boys or go to parties, wanted to keep her home for himself. Asked victim if she realized seriousness of charges she was making and she said she did. Said couldn't go home anymore and asked police protection.

Radioed for Women's and Children's Protective

11. Continuation of Officer's Report

Div. to pick up victim. Squad Car 613 with Sgt.
Arena and Officer Schwartz arrived app. 10:45 PM
and picked up victim.

Proceeded to home of suspect, arriving app. 10:55
PM. Mrs. Connie Nyland, wife of suspect, admitted
me to the house. Said could not talk to suspect as
he was upset because of lies daughter had told about
him. Explained that Suspect charged with serious
crime, and that writer must talk to him. Wife
finally agreed and said suspect was in basement of
home. Found suspect sitting in dark basement.
Advised him fully of his rights. He said he would
talk to me if I didn't turn the lights on, said was
ashamed to have me see his face. Said he did not
want an attorney and that he wanted to go to jail
because he was a monster and should not be allowed
loose.

Writer sat in dark with suspect and conducted
interrogation. Suspect admitted that victim was
telling the truth. Said he could not arouse his wife
when they were in bed together and that he had
turned to victim for sexual satisfaction. Said that
this had been going on for five years, since the
spring of 1965. Said sexual intercourse with victim
had occurred three or four times each month since
date of first occurrence. Suspect further stated
that he did not feel he could control self around
victim or other young girls and asked that he be
locked up.

Placed suspect under arrest and advised his wife
to secure attorney. Proceeded with suspect to
station for formal booking.

/S/ Robert Dolan
Badge No. 3121
1st Night Relief

As a result of Mr. Nyland's confession, he was charged with statutory rape, tried, convicted, and given a five-year sentence in the state penitentiary. The prison sentence was suspended on the condition that Mr. Nyland receive psychiatric care.

The confession, conviction, and attendant notoriety affected Mrs. Nyland extremely. She suffered frequent attacks of panic, and began to feel unreal, as if she were not really herself, but as if she were somehow standing apart and observing what she was doing. Her disturbance became so severe that she was hospitalized in a state mental hospital.

Alice was placed in the Wilson Shelter for Children and subsequently in a foster home. After several weeks Mrs. Nyland was discharged from the hospital and petitioned the juvenile court to regain custody of her daughter.

Prior to the custody hearing, the juvenile court counselor requested an evaluation by their psychiatric consultant, Dr. Breck Parker. Dr. Parker reported:

LAKEVIEW CHILD GUIDANCE CLINIC
1320 N. Alistaire Road
(963) 528-9934

July 14, 1970

Mrs. Alice Peabody
Juvenile Court Counselor
Children's Place of Detention

Dear Mrs. Peabody:
   Alice Nyland, who is a 14-year-old, unmarried student, was referred to me for an evaluation because her mother has petitioned the court to return the girl to the mother's custody. It is my understanding that Alice came to the attention of your agency because of her long-standing incestuous relationship with her father. Miss Nyland, together with her mother and grandmother, were interviewed at your agency on July 9, 1970.
   Mrs. Nyland presented a plan which entailed her going to

work and having Alice live with her grandmother in a tiny community in the southern part of the state. Alice's grandmother appeared to be an intelligent, kindly, well-intentioned individual who was horrified at the events that led to the disruption of Alice's family. She was quite willing to accept the girl into her home, but she was extremely cognizant of the potential gossip that would occur if an investigation as to the suitability of her home for placement of Alice were to be made in the town in which she lives. She stated repeatedly that she would do anything for Alice, but she vehemently opposed any suggestion that Alice might seek psychiatric help from any physician or agency in her community. She stated that she would gladly bring Alice to the city for such treatment, despite the fact that it would be rather expensive.

Alice's mother, Mrs. Connie Nyland, was distraught at our interview, and was tearful and disturbed over the circumstances in which she found herself. She stated that she had no notion that her husband was forcing sexual attentions upon her daughter despite the fact that this had gone on for approximately five years. She was unable to understand why her daughter had not confided in her and appeared to be quite bewildered and at a loss to explain any of the events which transpired. She was concerned about her own emotions and behavior, and she appeared to believe that I would think badly of her because of her depression and anxiety. She seemed desperately anxious to find someone in whom she could confide and appeared disappointed when I advised her that our relationship could not be considered a privileged communication, but that I was acting as an agent of the court. She was agreeable to suggestions that I made about the need for psychiatric care for her daughter, and she also agreed that she, herself, would benefit from such care.

Alice was rather wooden and emotionless during the interview. She described her sexual relationships with her father in a matter-of-fact way and did not appear at all anxious or depressed. Her description of the circumstances under which these acts of incestuous relations occurred was factual and convincing, and it was my feeling that the girl was being forthright and honest.

It was felt that a more intensive evaluation should be made of this girl than could be made at your agency. In consequence, a subsequent appointment was made, and Alice received a psychological evaluation of her intellectual and emotional status by Dr. Douglas of the County Mental Health Out-Patient Clinic.

Dr. Douglas reported that the results of the intelligence testing were rather surprising in that Alice's level of intellectual functioning appeared to be only in the dull normal range (IQ 85). There was nothing in the test results to suggest that Alice's level of functioning was impaired by brain injury or disease.

He further reported that the results of various personality tests would strongly suggest that Alice is suffering from a rather serious emotional disturbance. At times she has a very high level of anxiety, and at those times she is afraid she is losing her mind. She has many strange attitudes and false beliefs. She can be touchy and overly responsive to the opinions and demands of others, and she would appear to be easily led and influenced. Afterwards she is inclined to blame others for her own suggestibility and resultant difficulty. She often has feelings of unreality and bizarre and confused thinking which could lead to maladaptive behavior.

Despite the rather malignant results obtained from the tests Dr. Douglas administered, it should be remembered that this girl has been exposed to an extremely abnormal situation for several years, and it would be astonishing if her personality were not warped by her experiences. It would appear quite necessary to intervene at this time and provide her with psychotherapy that would help her to become a happier, better adjusted individual, and I would be inclined to see this as a primary goal.

I am most reluctant to make any recommendations that would further disrupt this family, but I feel that Alice needs immediate help from some competent source. There are no public agencies located anywhere close to the grandmother's home, and I would question if the financial resources of this family would permit such care to be obtained from any private source. In addition, I am certain that the grandmother wants to help, but I doubt if her attitude of repugnance toward the events that have occurred would be a positive factor in her relationship with Alice. Therefore, I would recommend that Alice be placed in a foster home in this city or in some other community supporting a public psychiatric agency so that she can receive the care that she so urgently needs. Therefore, it would seem that the only adequate solution would be to place the girl in a foster home and refuse to permit her to reside with her grandmother.

Very truly yours,

/S/ Breck Parker, M.D.

The hearing was held on August 7, 1970. The court appointed an attorney, Mr. Edward Grunden, to represent Mrs. Nyland. Deputy District Attorney Jerry Rusk, Dr. Parker, and Dr. Douglas were present.

STATE CIRCUIT COURT
Juvenile Division

In the Matter of	)	*No. 63,140*
Alice Nyland, minor	)	DISPOSITION AND ORDER

The above entitled matter having been heard on the *6th* day of *August 1970,* upon the petition of *Mrs. Connie Nyland* praying that an investigation be made of the circumstances concerning the above named minor, the following persons being present at the hearing: *Connie Nyland, mother; Grace Haver, grandmother; Alice Nyland, minor; Edward Grunden, attorney; Deputy District Attorney Jerry Rusk; witnesses.*

and it appearing to the Court, and the Court finding that:

1. Due notice of this proceeding has been given all persons interested herein.
2. The minor is a citizen of this county and under the jurisdiction of the Court.

The Court being fully advised in the premises:

NOW THEREFORE IT IS HEREBY ADJUDGED AND ORDERED:

   1. The evidence presented indicates that Mrs. Grace Haver is a woman of good character and is able to provide a suitable home for Alice Nyland.
   2. Alice Nyland is placed in the custody of Mrs. Grace Haver, her grandmother, and will reside in her home.

Dated this *7th* day of *August 1970.*

/S/ Patrick O'Mara

Judge

After the hearing Judge O'Mara relaxed with his colleagues and said: "That last case was a tough one. The two doctors are probably right, but I didn't have the heart to tell the grandmother that she shouldn't be able to keep the child."

The grandmother failed in her efforts to make a home for Alice. She was unable to rid her mind of endless speculation about the girl, and was unable to find any acceptable excuse in her own mind for the long incestuous relationship. She hoped that Alice was without fault in the matter and that Mr. Nyland was wholly to blame, but she could not understand why Alice had not asked her mother for help.

In her efforts to understand, she subjected Alice to long periods of questioning, asking how it happened, what was said, and what was done. This questioning troubled Alice. She was attempting to forget the whole affair, and the constant prying and searching kept her relationship with her father constantly present in her conscious mind. She really loved her father very much. She missed him and worried about him. She often regretted telling the police about their sexual involvement. Her grandmother's interrogations only increased her worries and regrets.

Her grandmother was determined that in the future Alice's conduct would be correct and proper. She continuously criticized Alice about her clothes, behavior, and appearance. She refused to let the girl wear any makeup and insisted that her behavior be prim and proper. She was also appalled by the notion that Alice should be allowed to date.

Alice remembered that Dr. Parker had recommended that she receive some sort of counseling or psychotherapy, so, feeling herself increasingly disturbed, she asked her grandmother to arrange for her to see a doctor. Her grandmother replied hotly: "We've got to keep this shameful thing to ourselves. We can't have everybody in town know what has been going on."

After two months Alice cashed several bad checks and used the money to run away.

Two weeks later she was apprehended and placed in custody. Her mother became acutely disturbed following this incident. It appeared that she was trying to become a young girl again. She wore mod clothes suitable for high school students and adopted many of the behavior patterns of the hippie community. She ate very little and found it difficult to sleep. She was finally found screaming on a downtown street. She was diagnosed as having Schizophrenia, Schizo-Affective Type, excited, and was committed to a state mental hospital once again.

Meanwhile, Mr. Nyland had complied with the terms of his suspended sentence and sought psychiatric care. He was a good patient in that he appeared to be highly motivated to change. He was quite talkative and seemed able to develop insights into the causes of his behavior. Apparently he had had long-standing feelings of inferiority; it was difficult for him to fully accept himself as being a capable, achieving adult. This offered a partial explanation as to why he sought sexual intercourse with his daughter while she was yet a child.

After six months of psychiatric treatment Nyland announced that he was "cured" and that he was not in need of any further treatment. His psychiatrist disagreed and attempted to point out to Mr. Nyland that he was just beginning to understand the causes of his deviant behavior and that further therapy was necessary. Mr. Nyland reluctantly agreed, but against the advice of his therapist he petitioned the court to have his daughter returned to his custody. The court refused his request.

In the course of these proceedings Mr. Nyland visited his wife at the state hospital several times. During their conversations he was repentent and often expressed a desire to be given a second chance. As Mrs. Nyland's condition improved, she was given weekend passes, and she and Mr. Nyland began to spend these weekends together. They found many fun things to do and came to realize that they still loved each other.

They decided to try to patch up their marriage. After Mrs. Nyland's discharge, they moved to a new neighborhood where their background was not known. Mr. Nyland found a new job. Mrs. Nyland's behavior seemed normal, and it appeared that they had made a successful marital adjustment.

Alice had been placed in a foster home while these events transpired and was doing reasonably well. Her school attendance was regular, her grades satisfactory, and her social life closely paralleled that of a normal girl. She frequently expressed concern for her mother and father, and her mother visited her frequently. These visits were always disturbing to Alice. After her mother left she often felt sorry for her mother and father.

Alice was receiving psychological counseling from Dr. Douglas while she was living in the foster home. After several sessions she found herself able to discuss her relationship with her father quite freely. She stated that she had always loved her father and that when she was a child he was always the one who had laughed and played with her and comforted her when things went wrong. Her mother had always been distant and uncommunicative. From infancy her father had dressed her, bathed her, and nursed her when she was ill. She felt no shame in his presence as she matured and often bathed while he was shaving in the same bathroom.

One evening while she and her father were alone together he discussed sex with her. He explained the necessity of sexual relationships for a man and told Alice that her mother would no longer permit him to have sexual relationships with her. He asked Alice if she would take Mrs. Nyland's place and be like a wife to him. She agreed.

Alice was both pleased and frightened. She was happy to be treated like a grown-up woman, but her father's sexual excitement frightened her, and the act itself hurt. However, over the years sexual intercourse with her father became a pleasant routine, and she came to cherish it.

When she became a freshman in high school, Alice began to question her relationship with her father and to feel that it was wrong. Boys would ask her for dates, but she felt she must refuse them. Other girls talked of their experiences with boys, and Alice felt shut out, not a part of the scene. She finally told her father that their relationship must stop.

But Mr. Nyland was not willing to stop. They discussed the matter frequently, and he finally attempted to rape her. That was the night she called the police. Despite this she was aware that her father continued to have a strong physical attraction for her.

After Mr. and Mrs. Nyland had been back together for approximately a year, they petitioned the court to have Alice returned to their home. A hearing was held on February 1, 1972. Attorney Wayne Hammill represented the parents, and Deputy District Attorney Jerry Rusk represented the state. Dr. Parker testified as to Mrs. Nyland's emotional instability. The psychiatrist who had been seeing Mr. Nyland for the past year and a half, Dr. John Hallay, testified to the effect that he would consider Mr. Nyland to still have many unresolved sexual problems. Dr. Douglas discussed Alice's many problems. All three vehemently opposed the notion of having Alice returned to her parents' custody.

STATE CIRCUIT COURT
Juvenile Division

In the Matter of   )   *No. 63,286*
  Alice Nyland, minor   )   DISPOSITION AND ORDER

The above entitled matter having been heard on the *1st* day of *February 1972*, upon the petition of *Leif and Connie Nyland* praying that an investigation be made of the circumstances concerning the above named minor, the following persons being present at the hearing: *Leif and Connie Nyland, parents; Alice Nyland, minor; Wayne Hammill, attorney; Deputy District Attorney Jerry Rusk, witnesses.*

and it appearing to the Court, and the Court finding that:
  1. Due notice of this proceeding has been given all persons interested herein.
  2. The minor is a citizen of this county and under the jurisdiction of the Court.
The Court being fully advised in the premises:

NOW THEREFORE IT IS HEREBY ADJUDGED
AND ORDERED:

  1. Alice Nyland will continue as a ward of this court.
  2. She will be returned to her parents' custody.
  3. This arrangement will be closely supervised by the Welfare Department.

Dated this *2nd* day of *February 1972*.

                    /S/ Chester Beshaw
                    —————————————————
                              Judge

Judge Beshaw was quite outspoken in his discussion of the decision with Jerry Rusk. "This is another case of head-shrinkers trying to keep people down," he said. "You have to learn to trust people and give them a chance. I don't know whether to believe half the stuff in this case anyway."

Two months after Alice had been returned to her parents' home, she confided to the supervising welfare worker that she thought she was pregnant. She named her father as the one who was responsible.

Mr. Nyland was arrested and once again admitted his guilt. An additional five-year sentence was imposed and he was confined in the state penitentiary. The welfare department which retained supervision of Alice arranged for a therapeutic abortion to be performed. As a result of this Alice suffered from a post-partum psychosis, and it was necessary for her to be placed in the state mental hospital. Shortly after, she was joined by her mother who had once again experienced a psychotic episode. The prognosis for recovery for both Alice and her mother is guarded.

Chapter 13 MARK AND JULIA

Sure, I burned the house down. The goddamned landlord
wouldn't fix the furnace, and we were freezing to death, so I
set the damned place on fire. What would you have done?

—A father's statement

Mark Adler was a jolly little boy. Until he started to school
he was greatly cherished and admired by his parents. Unfortunately, Mark was a dyslexic child; it was virtually impossible for him to learn to read or write. The personnel at
the school Mark attended were not equipped to accurately
diagnose this condition, so they attributed Mark's poor
school performance to lack of effort. They held several conferences with Mark's parents and explained that the boy
was intelligent and should be doing well in school, but it
appeared that he simply was not trying and as a result was
not learning to read. Mark's father's reaction to these difficulties was to punish him. Mark was told that he must get
reasonably good report cards in the future, that if he failed
to do so, he would be whipped. Consequently Mark was
regularly beaten six times a year, one thrashing for each
report card.

Mrs. Adler, Mark's mother, used a somewhat different
approach. She attempted to shame Mark into performing
better and continuously derided him, pointing out how
much better other children in the neighborhood were
doing in school. In her desire to make sure that Mark tried
harder, she developed the habit of admonishing him more
and more frequently, until it came to seem to Mark that he
was always being scolded by his mother.

After the first two dismal years in school the teachers
largely abandoned their efforts to instruct Mark and ignored him in class except when the occasion arose to make

189

some derogatory comment about his performance. His relationships with other children were influenced by the teachers' attitudes. The children quickly realized that the teacher had scorn and contempt for Mark, so they treated him similarly, making him the butt of many childish tricks and referring to him as "that dummy."

When he was nine Mark began to develop an explosive temper. He got in many fights in school, exploded and swore at his teacher, and stabbed with a putty knife an aunt who was teasing him. During these episodes Mark was completely out of control by others and unable to control himself. He was driven to strike out and hurt the object of his anger; until his temper subsided he was not capable of logical reasoning.

Mark's temper caused the other children to drastically modify their attitudes toward him. They no longer teased him or joked about him; instead they became cautious and treated him with fearful respect. Mark, of course, noticed this change and came to be rather proud of his temper. "They're all scared of me," he thought, "I don't have to take anything from any of them." The fear of the other children was a positive reinforcement of Mark's outbursts of temper; consequently his periods of rage became more frequent. He was often suspended from school, and his parents were completely baffled as to how to control him. When he reached high school, he was placed in special education classes.

Julia Knott's problems were less complex. She suffered from mild mental retardation. This condition was recognized in her early infancy, and few demands had been placed upon her. As a child she was allowed to do as she pleased. When she entered school she was immediately placed in special education classes where expectations for her achievement were low. As she grew older she developed into a spectacularly beautiful child, and in adolescence showed promise of becoming an extremely beautiful woman. When she entered high school, she was placed in the special education class with Mark. They became very close friends and before the end of the tenth grade had decided they were in love.

Since few demands had ever been made of Julia and she was accustomed to doing what she wanted to do when she wanted to do it, sex seemed like great fun to her. She could not comprehend any reason why she should not engage in sexual intercourse with whomever she happened to be with. This outraged Mark, and he frequently slapped and beat her when he learned that she had been with another boy. But this had little effect on Julia's behavior. Mark finally became completely outraged and accosted a boy who had been with Julia, beating him very severely. The police were called and Mark was arrested and taken to the Children's Place of Detention.

A hearing was scheduled in the Juvenile Court, and Mark was released in the custody of his father. Mark was afraid he would be sentenced to prison or to reform school, so he ran away.

Mark led a marginal existence for the next three years. He frequently found jobs in service stations or working on farms and ranches, but typically after a short period of time he would lose his temper and therefore his job. He drifted throughout the country and was frequently hungry and without a place to live. He thought of Julia often; while he occasionally met other girls, none of them was as beautiful as she and he was unable to form any real interest in any of them.

When he was 18, Mark returned to his parents' home. His father was overjoyed to see his son again, but he could not help but tell the boy that he looked like "a dirty, rotten bum." His mother was also pleased to see Mark and busily arranged for him to get new clothing, a haircut, and a thorough scrubbing. Mark was relieved to learn that the charge of assault against him had been dropped.

Mark found a job recapping second-hand tires. It was hot, irritating, dirty work, but he determined to stick it out. After he received his first paycheck, he went to Julia's home. Julia met him at the door. She was more beautiful than he had remembered. "Hi," Mark said, "I've come back for you, and I've got a good job. Let's get married."

Julia was thrilled at the notion of being a grown-up, married woman, free from the control of her mother and father. She and Mark left at once, went to an adjoining state where marriage licenses could easily be obtained, and were married by a justice of the peace. They returned to the city and began their life together in a small furnished room. Julia was pregnant within a month.

Life with Julia became very difficult for Mark. She had no notion of how to cook, clean or buy food. On several occasions she squandered the entire grocery allowance on candy, popcorn, and pretzels. If Mark admonished her, she sulked. This bothered Mark, but he soon learned to tickle her, and as she giggled, she regained her good humor. Nothing was ever changed, however; she would repeatedly make the same errors in judgment that disturbed her husband.

Before the child was born, Mark managed to acquire furniture, and they moved into a small, three-room apartment. Julia was frightened at the prospect of the labor that she must undergo to give birth. As the pregnancy advanced she was increasingly lugubrious. This irritated Mark, but he managed to avoid abusing her. However, his anger and irritation carried over to his job and blossomed into an assault on a customer.

Mark was arrested, tried, and convicted of assault and sentenced to four months in the county jail. During his imprisonment he continued to be easily irritated. His assaultive behavior resulted in an extension of his sentence.

While he was confined, Julia gave birth to Louisa. She proudly brought the baby to the jail to display to her father. The baby cried throughout the entire visit and irritated Mark so much that he insisted that Julia not bring the child to the jail again.

During Mark's imprisonment Julia was supported by the Welfare Department. A social caseworker made a routine visit to the home and was appalled. She reported:

> Mrs. Adler is a very poor housekeeper who simply does not know how to manage. She does not know how to cook, how to keep house, or how to care for a child. At the time of my visit the little girl, Louisa, was wearing a filthy nightshirt, dirty diapers, and despite the cold weather, she had no shoes or socks. Dirty clothes were heaped randomly throughout the apartment, and there were no clean clothes for the child or for its mother. Mrs. Adler appeared unconcerned about all of this and had no constructive plans for cleaning the apartment or washing the clothes. An investigation of the kitchen revealed that there was no food for the baby. The refrigerator contained several bottles of Coke and a dish of spoiled cottage cheese. The cupboards held several bags of potato chips and one box of pretzels—nothing else.
>
> Inasmuch as I feared for the welfare of the child under these conditions, I removed her from the home and placed her in the Wilson Shelter for Children. The juvenile court was notified of my actions, and a hearing will be scheduled. It should be noted that Mrs. Adler showed no concern whatsoever when I announced that I was taking the baby. It was my impression that she was rather pleased to be rid of the responsibility. I would recommend that a thorough investigation be made of this mother to determine if she can possibly be re-educated in such a manner as to make her able to care properly for her child.

A hearing was scheduled to determine what disposition was to be made of Louisa Adler. Prior to the hearing a case conference was held at which representatives of the

Juvenile Court, the Welfare Department, and the district attorney's office were present. It was agreed that it would be difficult to find a suitable foster home for an infant Louisa's age, and it was also conceded that it would be unlikely that the court would order that the child be taken from its mother. Therefore it was agreed that a part-time volunteer be assigned to work with Julia Adler in the hope that Mrs. Adler would learn better child rearing and housekeeping practices.

This plan was submitted to the court, and the judge agreed, incorporating it in his decision. Louisa was made a ward of the court, returned to her mother, and the Welfare Department assumed the responsibility of providing housekeeping guidance.

Subsequent to this, Mark was released from prison and returned home. Julia had been cooperative in working with the volunteer worker, and Mark was pleasantly surprised at the condition of the apartment. He thoroughly enjoyed getting acquainted with his daughter, and he happily played with her for long periods of time. He still found his wife very beautiful and very charming.

Mark decided that some of his problems were caused by the fact that he had never been able to find what he considered to be a decent job. Every place he had worked had been dirty, and the work was hard and disagreeable. He went to the State Employment Service and applied for help. The counselor to whom he was assigned was an interested, sympathetic person who interviewed Mark at length and determined to try to find some adequate employment for him. However, Mark was functionally illiterate. Except for the most menial jobs, it was very difficult to find an employer who would accept a person with such a handicap. The counselor eventually found Mark a job working with a janitorial service company.

Surprisingly Mark adjusted rather well to the new job.

The work consisted of cleaning office buildings; compared to his previous jobs, it was quite pleasant. He spent most of his time alone, sweeping and mopping floors, and there were few things to vex or irritate him. He felt that there was some possibility of promotion, and he was reasonably content.

After several quiet weeks Julia began to present problems for Mark and for the welfare worker. The welfare worker was a volunteer and had accepted the assignment with the sincere purpose of helping Julia to learn how to manage her household. But Julia came to look on the volunteer as a servant and complained if she was late or if she did not perform certain tasks Julia wanted her to do. There were frequent quarrels, and finally the volunteer quit in despair. This threw the burden of housekeeping entirely upon Julia; she reacted to the situation by doing little except complain about the absence of the volunteer worker.

Mark attempted to help Julia with the housework, but if he started to help, Julia immediately quit and contentedly amused herself watching television. This irritated Mark, but he found that nothing he could say or do would persuade Julia to adopt a more realistic attitude toward her responsibilities. She was simply a child and continued to behave in a very childlike way.

Mark worked from 3 to 11 p.m. When he got home in the evening, he usually found it necessary to wash the dishes, clean the house, and feed Louisa who had been put to bed hungry. It was usually two or three in the morning before he was able to go to bed. One morning while he was sleeping, Louisa began to cry, awakening him. As had happened so often in the past, his temper exploded. He jumped out of bed and ran into the child's room, striking her and breaking her jaw. When his temper subsided he was seriously alarmed about what had happened. He took Louisa

to Holy Angels Hospital, explaining Louisa's injuries by
saying she had fallen out of bed. His story was not believed
and the resident on duty called the police.

DEPARTMENT OF PUBLIC SAFETY
BUREAU OF POLICE
Officer's Report

1. Specific Crime	2. Place of Occurrence	3. Case No.
Assault – Child abuse	1173 Montgomery Rd.	67-9143

4. Date and Time Crime Occurred	5. Date and Time Crime Reported
6/13/67 – about 4:30 AM	6/13/67 – 5:15 AM

6. Victim's Name	7. Person Reporting Crime
Louisa Adler, minor, born 8/7/65	Seymour Harris, MD Holy Angels Hospital

8. Witnesses' Names	9. Suspect(s) Name
Suspect	Mark Adler (father of victim) 1173 Montgomery Rd.

10. Narrative of Crime, Describe Evidence, Summarize Details Not Given Above.

Received 219 from Radio Div. at 5:20 AM and
proceeded to Holy Angels Hosp. Was met on arrival
by complainant, Dr. Seymour Harris. Dr. Harris said
that they had a girl about two years old in the
emergency room who had a broken jaw and bruises on
her jaw that looked like she had been punched or hit
with some hard object. Said he was not satisfied
with story given by father, Mr. Mark Adler. Said
Mr. Adler said injuries occurred when child fell out
of bed onto floor, and that it couldn't have
happened that way.

Suspect and wife, Julia Adler, were in waiting

11. Continuation of Officer's Report

room. Advised them that I was a police officer and that I wanted to interrogate them about injury to their child. Advised them fully of their rights and they both said that they would talk to me. Took suspect to head nurse's office to take statement. Suspect said he was asleep and heard victim crying so went to her room and found her on the floor. Said her jaw seemed funny so he took her to hospital. Claimed that that was all he knew. Repeatedly denied that he had struck child. Also said wife had not hit child, that she was asleep and did not hear victim cry. Suspect got mad after I continued to question him and said he guessed police were out to get him. I asked if he had been in trouble with the law before, and he said that he had done time for an assault charge involving an adult. Denied that there had ever been problem of child abuse but admitted that his wife had had trouble caring for victim while he was in jail and that Juvenile Court and Welfare Dept had been involved.

Returned suspect to waiting room and returned with mother of victim, Julia Adler, to nurse's office. Mrs. Adler very upset and could not give reasonable account of what happened. She seemed simple, as if she were feeble minded. Said she was afraid of suspect, but said he never harmed her or victim. Then she said he had, then denied what she had just said.

Insufficient evidence to make arrest, so advised this couple that we would be in touch with them.

JUVENILE COURT AND WELFARE DEPT. SHOULD BE ADVISED OF THIS INCIDENT.

/S/ William Header
Badge 913
2nd Night Relief

In view of Mark's denial of responsibility and Julia's garbled account of the injury, it was decided by the district attorney's office that prosecution for assault was fruitless, but a dependency petition was prepared and submitted to the juvenile court. A hearing was held with Judge Patrick O'Mara presiding.

Attorney Donald Harrington who had been appointed to represent the parents, Deputy District Attorney Jerry Rusk, Mrs. Helen Wagner of the Welfare Department, and the entire Adler family were present. Mrs. Wagner testified as to the experience the Welfare Department had had with this family and expressed the opinion that Julia never could function effectively as a parent. Dr. Seymour Harris, of Holy Angels Hospital, testified as to the injuries received by the child and expressed the opinion that they could not have occurred in the manner described by the father. Despite this testimony, Louisa was returned to her parents' custody.

STATE CIRCUIT COURT
Juvenile Division

| In the Matter of |) | No. 86,347 |
| *Louisa Adler, minor* |) | DISPOSITION AND ORDER |

The above entitled matter having been heard on the *20th* day of *July 1967,* upon the petition of *Welfare Department* praying that an investigation be made of the circumstances concerning the above named minor, the following persons being present at the hearing: *Mark and Julia Adler, parents; Louisa Adler, minor; Mr. Donald Harrington, attorney; Deputy District Attorney Jerry Rusk; witnesses.*

and it appearing to the Court, and the Court finding that:

1. Due notice of this proceeding has been given all persons interested herein.

2. The minor is a citizen of this county and under the jurisdiction of the Court.

The Court being fully advised in the premises:

NOW THEREFORE IT IS HEREBY ADJUDGED
AND ORDERED:

1. Louisa Adler will be made a ward of this court.

2. She will be returned to her parents' custody under the supervision of the Welfare Department.

Dated this *21st* day of *July 1967*.

/S/ Patrick O'Mara
_____

Judge
_____

Judge O'Mara was quite worried about his decision and discussed it at some length with Mrs. Wagner after the hearing. He pointed out that there were not too many suitable foster homes available and that he thought that an intensive effort must be made by the Welfare Department to rehabilitate Mark and Julia. "These young people will go right on having children," he said, "and we can't take them all. We're going to have to find a way to teach this couple how to behave normally toward their children and toward each other."

The judge's prediction was accurate—Julia was pregnant again, and their second daughter, Tina, was born several months later. This increased the tension in the home, in that Julia remained unchanged, and Mark had to redouble his efforts to hold his job, care for Louisa and for the new baby, Tina. As might have been predicted, he once again lost his temper, this time severely injuring his boss. He was arrested, tried, and sentenced to ten months in the county jail. Julia and her little brood once again became recipients of assistance from the Welfare Department.

While Mark was in prison Julia met several other men and had sexual relations with all of them. As a result she became pregnant, and a son, Robert, was born shortly after Mark was released. This infuriated Mark, but he determined to stick with Julia and try to overlook her many shortcomings. He found a job working in a company that recapped used tires, the sort of job he disliked, but the only one he could find. They moved to a small cottage and attempted to resume a semblance of normal living. Unfortunately it was winter and the furnace in the cottage did not function properly. Mark frequently called the landlord and complained, but nothing was done. He grew madder and madder and attempted to find the landlord to "beat the hell out of him." He was unable to locate the landlord. As his anger increased he returned home and seriously beat Julia and the children, including the infant, Robert. Julia, who was badly hurt and extremely frightened, took the three children to the County Hospital.

All three children were examined there, but there were no indications of broken bones or serious injuries. It was discovered, however, that Louisa and Tina had pneumonia which had been aggravated by lack of adequate heat and nutrition. The resident on duty at the County Hospital notified the police of the child abuse and neglect.

DEPARTMENT OF PUBLIC SAFETY
BUREAU OF POLICE
Officer's Report

1. Specific Crime	2. Place of Occurrence	3. Case No.
Assault	1173 Montgomery Rd.	74-6601

4. Date and Time Crime Occurred Jan. 19, 1970 about 2:30 PM	5. Date and Time Crime Reported Jan. 19, 1970 – 3:45 PM
6. Victim's Name Julia Adler, minor children Louisa, Tina, and Robert Adler	7. Person Reporting Crime Stanley Vogt, MD Receiving Room, County Hospital
8. Witnesses' Names Victims	9. Suspect(s) Name Mark Adler 1173 Montgomery Rd.

10. Narrative of Crime, Describe Evidence, Summarize Details Not Given Above.

Received 219 from Radio Div. and went to County Hospital where I contacted Dr. Stanley Vogt who showed victims to me. Julia Adler, mother, appeared badly beaten about face and head, had been bleeding from nose, mouth and one ear. Children's faces red and puffy, Tina Adler bleeding from nose. Dr. Vogt advised that Julia Adler had broken nose, possible ruptured ear drum, and several loose teeth. Phoned Radio Div. and arranged for Detective Div. to take pictures of injured victims.

Spoke to Julia Adler and asked what had happened. She said suspect, her husband, had inflicted injuries. Asked if she would prefer charges and she said she would. Contacted Radio Div. again and arranged for Detective Div. to take formal statement from victim, Julia Adler, at time pictures were taken.

Proceeded to 1173 Montgomery St. and found suspect waiting on porch. Said he had been expecting the police. Writer advised him that a crime was under investigation and advised him of his rights. He said he would talk to me, that it didn't make any difference if he did it now or later. Said he lost

11. Continuation of Officer's Report

```
his temper easily and that he was mad at his
landlord and when he was mad he got mad at everybody,
and that was how he happened to beat up his wife and
children. Said he was sorry but that he couldn't
control self when he was angry.
    Placed suspect under arrest and proceeded to
station house for formal booking.
                         /S/ Donald Hickman
                             Badge No. 599
                             1st Nite Relief
```

As a result of the police investigation a petition was prepared alleging that the parents of the Adler children had
failed to provide them with the care, guidance, and protection necessary for their physical, mental, and emotional
well-being and had subjected them to acts of abuse. Because of Julia's statement, Mark had been arrested,
charged with assault and child neglect, and had subsequently been released on bail. When he returned home he
found Julia cold and shivering, sitting in an unheated
house. He became enraged and made Julia wait in the
front yard while he gathered what combustibles he could
find and set fire to the house. It was completely destroyed.

Mark was once again arrested and charged with arson.
Because the bail was high and he was unable to raise
money for his release, he remained in jail.

Prior to the hearing Mrs. Wagner of the Welfare Department suggested that Julia was emotionally disturbed, and
the judge ordered that she receive a psychiatric or psychological evaluation. This was done by Dr. Douglas of the
County Mental Health Out-Patient Clinic. Dr. Douglas reported: "Mrs. Julia Adler was interviewed and tested on
February 15, 1970. This unfortunate woman suffers from
mild mental retardation and is not intellectually equipped

to perform many of the duties expected of a wife and mother. In addition, she has an inadequate personality and as a result makes inappropriate or ineffectual responses to most emotional, social, and intellectual situations in which she finds herself. She is frequently tired and dispirited. She not only is incapable, but has no motivation to strive or to learn, and she has no real desire to improve her situation in life. It is very difficult for me to conceive any situation in which this woman could function adequately as a wife and mother."

A hearing was held on March 3, 1970. Mr. John Huffman, attorney, was appointed to represent Mrs. Adler. Mrs. Wagner of the Welfare Department, Deputy District Attorney Jerry Rusk, and Dr. Douglas were present.

STATE CIRCUIT COURT
Juvenile Division

In the Matter of	)	*No. 77,649*
Adler children	)	DISPOSITION AND ORDER

The above entitled matter having been heard on the *3rd* day of *March 1970*, upon the petition of *Welfare Department* praying that an investigation be made of the circumstances concerning the above named minor, the following persons being present at the hearing: *Julia Adler, mother; the Adler children; Mr. John Huffman, attorney; Deputy District Attorney Jerry Rusk; witnesses.*

and it appearing to the Court, and the Court finding that:

1. Due notice of this proceeding has been given all persons interested herein.
2. The minor is a citizen of this county and under the jurisdiction of the Court.

The Court being fully advised in the premises:

NOW THEREFORE IT IS HEREBY ADJUDGED
AND ORDERED:

*1. Mrs. Julia Adler has been unable to provide proper care
for her children, Louisa, Tina, and Robert Adler.*
*2. The children will continue as wards of this court and
will be surrendered to the Welfare Department for foster
home placement.*

Dated this *4th* day of *March 1970*.

/S/ *Henry J. Puttman*
_____
Judge

All of the Adler children were placed in a foster home.
Unfortunately the foster parents were compulsive, demanding individuals who found the behavior of Louisa un-
acceptable and requested that she be placed elsewhere.
Inasmuch as the judicial order did not permit the children
to be separated, all of them were moved to another foster
home. At this time Mrs. Wagner left the Welfare Department to return to school and was replaced by Mrs. Alice
Harrington.

Mrs. Harrington was a kindly woman who was deeply
endowed with the notion that any individual was capable
of reform, no matter what his intellectual capacity, his
personality characteristics, or his past history. Her lack
of formal training permitted her to entertain such beliefs.
She saw her primary goal as finding ways to reunite the
Adler children with their parents. She frequently visited
Julia, who was living in a small apartment, and developed
a friendly relationship with her.

During this period Mark was on a work release program
at the penal institution, which meant that he was per-

mitted to leave the institution to work each day and that he received weekend passes to visit his wife. Mark, who was currently working at a service station, favorably impressed Mrs. Harrington. After several weeks Mrs. Harrington returned Robert to Julia's custody without the approval of the court. Julia mastered all her resources and did a fairly adequate job of caring for the one child. Mrs. Harrington was greatly encouraged.

Meanwhile there was an incident at the service station. In a rage at a customer, Mark beat out the windshield of his car with a tire iron. His work release privileges were revoked and he was incarcerated in a maximum security institution.

Julia was saddened by this event and missed Mark's visits. To compensate, Mrs. Harrington petitioned the court to return her children to her. In the petition Mrs. Harrington stated that Julia was now an adequate mother and that the father was no longer in the home. As a result of the petition the children were returned to Julia's custody and a volunteer housekeeping aide was assigned to her. This aide visited Julia for a half day three days a week and managed to help Julia regulate her money and adequately care for the children. This situation prevailed for two years, at which time Mark was paroled.

Upon his return home, Mark was hostile and embittered. He was alone in the bedroom with Julia when Robert began to cry. He lost his temper, rushed from the bedroom, and grabbed Robert by the heels. He swung the boy, beating his head against a table. Robert died.

Louisa and Tina are now in a foster home. Julia is living on welfare assistance and Mark is serving a life sentence in the penitentiary.

Chapter 14 "TO TRIUMPH OVER TRAGEDY"

These tragedies could have been avoided. The fact that they did occur illustrates the inadequacies of our courts and social agencies in their attempts to cope with the problems of abused or neglected children. If children are to be rescued from the barbarism of abusive parents, certain mandatory steps will have to be taken.

1. Our present judicial procedures must be modified to include improved reporting procedures; determination of questions of fact by a jury, and legal counsel for the abused child.

2. More highly qualified persons must be found to serve as juvenile court judges.

3. Hearings involving child abuse and neglect should be held in an open court to which the press is admitted.

4. Our philosophical assumptions as to the rights of parents must be re-examined. Children are not pieces of property belonging to their parents, but rather human beings whose welfare should be most carefully protected. In many cases all parental rights should be terminated.

5. Alternate types of placement for abused children must be explored.

A Child's Bill of Rights

The first requirement for helping abused children is an adequate reporting law. Such a law should protect the often frightened person making the complaint; therefore, anonymous complaints should be accepted. Investigations of all complaints should be made immediately. Because in most communities only the police have the facilities for making immediate, on-the-spot checks of complaints 24 hours a day, they might well provide the central bureau to which complaints could be made.

Reporting should be mandatory for any person who knows of child abuse or neglect; those who fail to report occurrences of child abuse should be liable to both criminal and civil action. There should be no privileged communication between parents and physicians where abuse is alleged, and persons making complaints should be free of any threat of legal retaliation.

As an example, a reporting section of a child protection law might read:

1) Abuse of a child shall consist of any of the following acts: (a) inflicting unnecessarily severe corporal punishment upon a child; (b) inflicting upon a child unnecessary suffering or pain, either mental or physical; (c) habitually tormenting or vexing a child; (d) any willful act of omission or commission whereby unnecessary pain and suffering, whether mental or physical, is caused or permitted to be inflicted upon a child; or (e) exposing a child to unnecessary hardship, fatigue, or mental or physical strains that may tend to injure the health or physical or moral well-being of such child.

2) Neglect of a child shall consist of any of the following acts by anyone having the custody or control of the child: (a) willfully failing to provide proper and sufficient food, clothing, maintenance, regular school education as required by law, medical attention and surgical treatment, and a clean and proper home; or (b) failure to do or permit to be done any act necessary for the child's physical or moral well-being.

3) Any person having reasonable cause to believe that a child is being abused or neglected as defined by this act shall immediately report the suspected abuse or neglect to the law enforcement agency having jurisdiction. Anyone participating in the making of such a report shall be presumed to be acting in good faith, and in so doing shall be immune from any liability, civil or criminal.

Neither the physician-patient privilege nor the husband-wife privilege shall be grounds for failure to report suspected child abuse or neglect.

Any person failing to comply with this section shall be guilty of a misdemeanor.

4) Law enforcement agencies receiving reports of suspected abuse or neglect shall endeavor to ascertain the name and address of the complainant, but will respect the right of the complainant to remain anonymous. If possible, information as to the name and address of the abused or neglected child, his age, his present whereabouts, the names and addresses of his parents or other persons responsible for his care, the nature and extent of the abuse or neglect, other children in the home who may be threatened with abuse or neglect, and any other information that may be deemed helpful shall be obtained.

A full investigation of the alleged abuse or neglect shall be made immediately upon the receipt of the complaint. In the event that law enforcement officers are denied access to the home or place where the child is kept, the report of suspected child abuse will be grounds for the issuance of a search warrant.

5) If, upon investigation, the law enforcement officers find reasonable grounds to believe that abuse or neglect has occurred, they shall immediately remove the child and place it in the custody of the medical or social agency deemed most suitable for the welfare of the child. They shall make a full report of their findings and actions to the district attorney, the court having juvenile jurisdiction, and to the Welfare Department.

After the complaint has been made and investigated, certain legal procedures are activated. Those now in effect have their origin in the first juvenile court, which was founded in Cook County, Illinois in 1899. This Chicago court was established because of the growing distaste for the notion that a child should be treated as a common criminal. Children over seven had been tried in adult courts. In the nineteenth century a child offender was occasionally hanged, and others were confined in prisons with adult offenders.

In establishing the first juvenile court it was argued that a child should not be treated as a criminal but instead as a child who should be rehabilitated rather than punished.

Unique judicial procedures were established. The cases were heard in a separate courtroom; the records of juvenile offenders were kept apart from those of adult offenders; indictments were not sought; warrants for arrest were not issued; and trial by jury was eliminated.

The desirability of having juvenile courts was apparent, and the model of the Chicago juvenile court was rapidly emulated, until today similar courts and procedures are found in every state.

The law that established the first juvenile court in Chicago provided that the jurisdiction of the court should extend to neglected and abused children as well as to children of criminal or asocial behavior, a provision that was adopted by other states. As a result, when parents are accused of abuse or neglect, many customary legal procedures are not followed. The facts in the case are not determined by a jury but by a judge. The abused child is not represented by counsel. The press is usually excluded. The judge has wide latitude to decide the fate of the child, and as we have shown, is often astoundingly ill-qualified to exercise his dictatorial powers.

All these deviations from usual legal procedure were originally adopted to *shield the child* from treatment as a common criminal. In child abuse cases, however, they *shield the parent*. The notion may be valid that regular criminal court procedures should not apply when a child is charged with an offense, but there is no rational or legal justification for affording abusive parents special protection that is not afforded to the pettiest criminal.

The adversary nature of judicial cases involving child abuse and neglect makes it mandatory that all parties involved in the dispute be represented by counsel. Trial lawyers are a curious breed; they champion the individuals who retain them, with an apparent unconcern for justice or the rights of other individuals who might be involved.

They are legal gunfighters who shoot from the hip without regard for anyone except their clients.

The child is the person most affected by decisions in dependency cases, but he is never represented by counsel. The parents' attorney is *their* adroit champion, but there is no one whose sole concern it is to insure that the child's rights and interests are adequately represented. In theory the district attorney's office is charged with presenting the case against the parents, but these overworked attorneys are not really advocates of the child. In every case where child abuse or neglect is alleged, a lawyer should be appointed to represent the child, thus insuring that the child, as well as its parents, will have a champion interested only in him and his welfare. Any child abuse statute should contain a section similar in intent to the following:

> At the time the child and the parents or persons causing the abuse or neglect are brought before the court the court shall advise them of the reason for their appearance, the nature of the proceedings, and the possible results of the proceedings. The court shall appoint an attorney to represent the child, and shall advise the parents that they are entitled to have an attorney to represent them. If they do not have funds with which to retain an attorney, the court will appoint an attorney to represent them.
>
> The attorney for the child and the attorney for the parents shall have the right to question witnesses and to subpoena witnesses on behalf of their clients.

In dependency cases such as we have been discussing, the facts to be determined are whether or not the parents have been unfit, whether abuse or neglect has occurred while the child was in their custody. We have a long legal tradition, supported by appropriate statutes, requiring that questions of fact be determined by a jury. The use of a jury was instituted to protect defendants from capricious, dictatorial judges acting as agents of the king. A jury of peers was thought to be a group of people who would weigh the facts impartially and reach a verdict on the basis of the evidence presented, free of external influence.

The kings are gone, but capricious, dictatorial judges remain. Anyone accused of a felony has the right to a jury trial. If the criminal is so protected, certainly similar protection should be given to a helpless child.

In Chapter 2 we described Judge Chester Beshaw, a bigoted old man who refused to consider facts that reflected adversely on the Maxwell parents. As a result he returned the children to parental custody and a life of continuing abuse.

In Chapter 6 we discussed Patrick Sweeny, a violent, unpredictable father who suffered irreversible brain damage. The judge, Robert Cochran, returned Mr. Sweeny's son to his custody because he feared the political consequences of his decision if he retained the boy in the foster home where he was doing so well.

It would seem apparent that if these dependency cases are to be determined by the facts presented, a jury must be employed to determine the facts as in other judicial procedures. Therefore, an adequate child abuse statute should contain a section similar to the following:

> All hearings or trials in which child abuse or neglect is alleged shall be heard by a jury. This provision shall not be waived except upon the request of the attorney representing the child and the attorney representing the parents or others having custody of the child.

Judges, Juries and Open Courts

The quality of juvenile court judges must be upgraded. In many states these judges are county officials, and the counties cannot offer salaries that will attract qualified people. In the last survey by the National Council of Juvenile Court Judges, previously cited, it was learned that 50 percent of the juvenile court judges earned no more than

$12,000 a year; 27 percent earned no more than $8,000 a year. Such salaries are not likely to attract competent officials.

Juvenile courts should be state courts, with full-time, well-paid, appointed judges. In smaller states these could be circuit courts, which could conduct hearings in several different localities. The judges appointed should have as a minimal requirement an undergraduate degree and preferably should have graduated from law school and have been admitted to the bar. Continuing education, preferably in the behavioral sciences, should be encouraged, perhaps with salary increases as a reward for further graduate study.

We have argued that the facts in each case of child abuse or neglect should be determined by a jury. We would also argue that if the jury finds that abuse or neglect has occurred, the judge should have the benefit of expert advice before he makes his decision. In each case a psychiatrist, a psychologist, or a qualified social worker should be available to consult with the judge and advise him of the probable consequences of the various decisions under consideration.

Since Thomas Jefferson many diverse and respected individuals have argued that if a democracy is to function, the public must be informed as to how agencies of the government are conducting their affairs. Many of us today are outraged at the secrecy that surrounds the Presidency, the Pentagon, and other branches of our government. The secrecy that surrounds juvenile court proceedings is no less outrageous. The press should be admitted to every juvenile court hearing unless counsel for both the parents and the child agree that there is a compelling reason for conducting the hearing privately.

It is the parents, not the children, who are being judged in dependency hearings. If they were charged with drunken driving, embezzlement, or any other crime, they would be exposed to the glare of publicity. There is no logical reason for those who have abused their children, a particularly despicable offense, to be shielded from the news media. If the court proceedings described here had been made public, the resulting outcry might have produced much-needed reforms.

Foster Homes, Adoption or Further Abuse

In extreme cases it becomes apparent to any reasonable observer that the parents should never be permitted to have custody of their children. The risk of further abuse or neglect is too great.

For example, Carl Maxwell, whose savage behavior toward his stepchildren was discussed in Chapter 2, is psychotic. He has Schizophrenia, Paranoid Type; he is sure he is right and that the rest of the world is wrong. He is not interested in any sort of psychiatric treatment and would strongly resent the notion that he has any emotional or intellectual deficits. He does not want to change, and it is highly unlikely he ever will. He should never be trusted with the responsibility of raising children.

Mr. and Mrs. Tompkins, described in Chapter 5, have extremely disordered personalities. Mrs. Tompkins is completely inadequate and Mr. Tompkins is a ruthless, uncaring egocentric. Despite the death of one of their children and the serious neglect of the others, they have once again been permitted the unsupervised custody of an infant. This couple can never become adequate parents.

Patrick Sweeny (Chapter 6) has suffered brain damage from which he will never recover. His impulsive, assaultive behavior is not susceptible to modification, and he can never function adequately in any capacity, including that of a father.

Depriving parents of their children is a repugnant decision, inasmuch as the notions of absolute right and complete competence of parents are deeply rooted. We tend to believe that a child belongs to its parents, much like a piece of property. In addition, if a child is to be taken permanently from the home, alternate placements are often not satisfactory.

The usual placement is in a foster home. Most foster parents are sincere and well meaning but are often not knowledgeable as to how to relate to a child who has been abused or neglected. Other foster parents are simply running a poorly paying business—child care—and are without warmth or concern for the foster children placed in their homes.

Foster home placements are often not long term. For one reason or another, foster parents will decide to stop caring for foster children or give up on a particular child. The result is that children taken from their parents are often placed in a succession of foster homes with no real security and no sense of belonging and of being loved. In such cases it should be permissible for the court to put these children up for adoption, so that they would be in a stable home situation and could experience the love and warmth of parents who care.

Some New Directions

Alternate types of placement may soon be available. Organizations such as The Villages are being formed to provide a stable, loving, home-like atmosphere for neglected or predelinquent children. The Villages, Inc. is a nonprofit organization founded as a result of spadework done by the Menninger Foundation of Topeka, Kansas. In each Village there are cottages housing 10 to 12 boys and girls. There is a set of trained foster parents permanently assigned to each cottage. Expert psychiatric and psychological consultants are available, but they do not intrude on the establishment of a positive parent-child relationship. Everything possible is done to make the child feel loved and wanted and that he is a person of worth. Placements are usually for long periods; a child may remain until he graduates from high school. Such home-like, family settings would be ideal for the rehabilitation of abused or neglected children.

This chapter is intended to recommend procedures that would salvage children after abuse has occurred. Obviously it would be preferable if steps could be taken to prevent such abuse. Action programs such as C.A.L.M. (Child Abuse Listening Mediation) are examples of how concerned citizens can effectively intervene in this area.

C.A.L.M. was founded in 1970 by Claire W. Miles, a registered nurse. Mrs. Miles determined to do something about child abuse. She installed a private, unlisted phone in her home in Santa Barbara, California and began advertising in the personal column of a local newspaper. The advertisement requested anyone who knew of an abused or neglected child to call her number. She received 28 calls the first month, in some instances from abusive parents themselves. In every case an attempt was made to provide preventive measures.

C.A.L.M. has now grown to an organization that includes 21 volunteer workers with appropriate psychiatric and psychological assistance. When a call is received, a volunteer visits the home, evaluates the situation, and takes whatever action may be necessary. In some instances it is sufficient if the volunteer acts as a nonjudgmental, empathetic listener to a worried, harrassed parent. In other cases referrals are made to appropriate social or judicial agencies. No call for help goes unanswered; as a result, many parents are able to find ways of coping with their problems, and child abuse is avoided. Similar efforts are being made elsewhere, and a variety of "hot lines" have been established in several states.

Parents Anonymous, an organization of abusive parents, has formed chapters in several areas. This is a self-help organization similar to Alcoholics Anonymous. Parent members report that they are learning ways to cope with their anger and frustration other than abusing their children.

All parents, and especially mothers, need some relief from what can be endless day-after-day irritating behavior by their children. Most mothers could cope with their children if they had adequate breathing spells. Our daycare center programs should be greatly expanded, and every mother should have access to such a center where she could leave her children in the care of competent personnel and give her some release from her endless responsibilities.

The Time is Now

Obviously the changes we have recommended would require action by state legislatures to change existing laws. Such action is possible. Child abusers are not popular people; there are no organized lobbies, such as often paralyze state legislatures, to work against constructive proposals for improving the protection given children.

This is a propitious time for change. Personnel of most social agencies concerned with abuse and neglect of children are dissatisfied with present laws and procedures. The pediatric departments of many hospitals and medical schools have special committees to study the problem. A recent court case sought civil damages because of deficient reporting and investigation of assaults on a child. As a result, the public is becoming increasingly aware and alarmed.

Concerned individuals or groups could make contact

with agencies listed in the Appendix to determine the status of child abuse and neglect laws in their communities. Contact can be made with state senators and congressmen, and their assistance can be solicited for changing existing laws that are inadequate. It is often a tedious process, but it can be done—if we care.

APPENDIX

A limited list of agencies that are concerned with the problems of child abuse and neglect appears below. Obviously it is impossible to include every county welfare agency or similar local public unit or private agency. We have endeavored, however, to include those agencies of which we are aware that have indicated a special interest in child protection. The state agencies listed are those with primary legal responsibility to provide protective services to children, but agencies on the county or city level may actually provide the services.

NATIONAL
American Humane Association
P.O. Box 1266,
Denver, Colorado 80201
This is a national association of individuals and agencies working to prevent neglect, abuse, and exploitation of children.

Child Welfare League of America, Inc.
67 Irving Place
New York, New York 10003
This is a national, privately supported organization which devotes its efforts to the improvement of services to deprived, neglected, and dependent children throughout the United States.

ALABAMA
Bureau of Family and Children's Services
Department of Pensions and Security
Administrative Building
64 North Union Street
Montgomery, Alabama 36104

ALASKA
Alaska Children's Service
4600 Abbott Road
Anchorage, Alaska 99507

ARIZONA
Family & Child Welfare Services Division
Arizona State Department of Public Welfare
1624 West Adams Street
Phoenix, Arizona 85007

ARKANSAS
Division of Child Welfare
Arkansas State Department of Public Welfare
Box 1437
Little Rock, Arkansas 72203

CALIFORNIA
Department of Social Welfare
State of California Health and Welfare Agency
744 P Street
Sacramento, California 95814

Los Angeles Department of Public Social Services
Family and Children's Services
1801 West Valley Boulevard
Alhambra, California 91803

Pasadena Welfare Bureau
238 East Union Street
Pasadena, California 91101

Parents Anonymous
2009 Farrell Avenue
Redondo Beach, California 90278

COLORADO
Family & Children's Services
Division of Public Welfare
1575 Sherman Street
Denver, Colorado 80203

Colorado University Medical Center
Denver, Colorado 80910

Jewish Family & Children's Service of Denver
1375 Delaware Street
Denver, Colorado 80204

CONNECTICUT
Connecticut Welfare Department
1000 Asylum Avenue
Hartford, Connecticut 06115

Connecticut Child Welfare Association
P.O. Box 3007
New Haven, Connecticut 06515

DART Committee
Department of Pediatrics
Yale-New Haven Hospital
789 Howard Avenue
New Haven, Connecticut 06504

DELAWARE
State Department of Health & Social Services
Division of Social Services
3000 Newport Gap Pike
Wilmington, Delaware 19808

FLORIDA
The Division of Family Services
5920 Arlington Expressway
Jacksonville, Florida 32211

GEORGIA
Division of Family and Children Services
Georgia Department of Human Resources
State Office Building
Atlanta, Georgia 30334

HAWAII
Public Welfare Division
Department of Social Services and Housing
P.O. Box 339
Honolulu, Hawaii 96809

IDAHO
Family & Children's Services
State Department of Social and Rehabilitation Services
P.O. Box 1189
Boise, Idaho 83701

ILLINOIS
Illinois Department of Children and Family Services
524 South Second Street
Springfield, Illinois 62706

Juvenile Protective Association
12 East Grand
Chicago, Illinois 60619

Chicago Child Care Society
5467 South University
Chicago, Illinois 60615

Illinois Children's Home and Aid Society
1122 North Dearborn Street
Chicago, Illinois 60610

INDIANA
Division of Social Services
Department of Public Welfare
100 North Senate Avenue—Room 701
Indianapolis, Indiana 46204

Lutheran Social Services, Inc.
330 Madison Street
Fort Wayne, Indiana 46802

IOWA
Department of Social Services
Lucas State Office Building
Des Moines, Iowa 50319

Black Hawk County Department of Social Service
Court House
Waterloo, Iowa 50703

Cerro Gordo County Department of Social Service
Court House
Mason City, Iowa 50401

Dubuque County Department of Social Service
Conlin Building—3rd Floor
1472 Central Avenue
Dubuque, Iowa 52001

Johnson County Department of Social Service
538 Central Avenue
Iowa City, Iowa 52240

Linn County Department of Social Service
400—3rd Ave. S.E.
Cedar Rapids, Iowa 52401

Polk County Department of Social Services
112—116 Eleventh Street
Des Moines, Iowa 50309

Pottawattamie County Department of Social Services
231 Pearl Street
Council Bluffs, Iowa 51502

Scott County Department of Social Services
808 West River Drive
Davenport, Iowa 52801

Wapello County Department of Social Services
Court House
Ottumwa, Iowa 52501

Woodbury County Department of Social Services
411 Seventh Street
Sioux City, Iowa 51101

Child Abuse and Severe Neglect Committee
Court House
Waterloo, Iowa 50703

Child Abuse Committee
Department of Pediatrics
University Hospitals
Iowa City, Iowa 52240

KANSAS
Division of Services to Children, Youth & Their Families
State Department of Social Welfare
State Office Building
Topeka, Kansas 66612

Kansas Child Protective Services, Inc.
P.O. Box 16105
Wichita, Kansas 67202

KENTUCKY
Department of Child Welfare
403 Wapping Street
Frankfort, Kentucky 40601

Metropolitan Social Services Department
522 West Jefferson
Louisville, Kentucky 40203

Fayette County Children's Bureau
115 Cisco Road
Lexington, Kentucky 40504

LOUISIANA
Department of Public Welfare
P.O. Box 44065
Baton Rouge, Louisiana 70804

MAINE
Department of Health and Welfare
Augusta, Maine 04330

MARYLAND
Social Services Administration
1315 St. Paul Street
Baltimore, Maryland 21202

Massachusetts Department of Public Welfare
600 Washington Street
Boston, Massachusetts 02111

Jewish Family and Children's Service
31 North Chardon Street
Boston, Massachusetts 02114

Massachusetts Society for the Prevention of Cruelty to Children
43 Mt. Vernon Street.
Boston, Massachusetts 02108

Children's Advocates
21 James Street
Boston, Massachusetts 02118

Children's Hospital
Trauma X Committee
295 Longwood Avenue
Boston, Massachusetts 02115

Trauma X Committee
Boston City Hospital
Harrison Avenue
Boston, Massachusetts 02111

MICHIGAN
State Department of Social Services
Bureau of Family and Children's Services
Lewis Cass Building
Lansing, Michigan 48913

Jewish Family and Children's Services
10801 Curtis
Detroit, Michigan 48221

Catholic Social Services of the Diocese of Grand Rapids
300 Commerce Building
Grand Rapids, Michigan 49502

D. A. Blodgett Homes for Children
805 Leonard N.E.
Grand Rapids, Michigan 49503

Catholic Social Services of St. Clair County
2601—13th Street
Port Huron, Michigan 48060

Child and Family Service of Saginaw County
1110 Howard Street
Saginaw, Michigan 46801

MINNESOTA
Minnesota Department of Public Welfare
Centennial Building
St. Paul, Minnesota 55108

MISSISSIPPI
Family and Children's Services
Mississippi State Department of Public Welfare
P.O. Box 4321, Fondren Station
Jackson, Mississippi 39216

MISSOURI
Family and Children's Services
State Department of Public Health and Welfare
State Office Building
Jefferson City, Missouri 65101

Social Service Department
Cardinal Glennon Hospital
1465 South Grand Boulevard
St. Louis, Missouri 63104

MONTANA
Social and Rehabilitation Services
Social Services Division
P.O. Box 1723
Helena, Montana 59601

NEBRASKA
Division of Social Services
Nebraska Department of Public Welfare
1526 K Street—Fourth Floor
Lincoln, Nebraska 68508

Nebraska Committee for Children and Youth
State House—Eleventh Floor, N.W.
Lincoln, Nebraska 68501

NEVADA
Nevada State Welfare Division
201 South Fall Street
Carson City, Nevada 89701

Washoe County Welfare Department
1205 Mill Street
Reno, Nevada 89502

Clark County Juvenile Court Services
East Bonanza Road and Pecos Drive
Las Vegas, Nevada 89107

NEW HAMPSHIRE
Bureau of Child and Family Services
Department of Health and Welfare
1 Pillsbury Street
Concord, New Hampshire 03301

NEW JERSEY
New Jersey Bureau of Children's Services
Department of Institutions and Agencies
163 West Hanover Street

Trenton, New Jersey 08625
Child Service Association
284 Broadway
Newark, New Jersey 07104

NEW MEXICO
New Mexico Health and Social Services Department
Social Services Division
P.O. Box 2348
Santa Fe, New Mexico 87501

NEW YORK
Protective Services Unit
Bureau of Community Services
State Department of Social Services
1450 Western Avenue
Albany, New York 12203

Select Committee on Child Abuse
270 Broadway
New York, New York 10007

Mayor's Task Force on Child Abuse
St. Vincent's Hospital
Seventh Avenue and West 11th Street
New York, New York 10003

Brooklyn Society for the Prevention of Cruelty to Children
67 Schermerhorn Street
Brooklyn, New York 11201

Manhattan Society for the Prevention of Cruelty to Children
110 East 71st Street
New York, New York 10021

Bronx Society for the Prevention of Cruelty to Children
370 East 149 Street
Bronx, New York 10455

Queensboro Society for the Prevention of Cruelty to Children
105-16 Union Hall Street
Jamaica, New York 11433

Monroe County Committee on Child Abuse
260 Crittenden Boulevard
Rochester, New York 14620

Onondaga County Child Abuse Committee
c/o United Community Chest and Council
107 James Street
Syracuse, New York 13202

Children's Aid & the Society for the Prevention of Cruelty to Children of Erie County, New York
330 Delaware Avenue
Buffalo, New York 14202

Jewish Family Service of Erie County
775 Main Street
Buffalo, New York 14203

Louise Wise Services
12 East 94th Street
New York, New York 10028

NORTH CAROLINA
Family & Children's Services Section
Department of Social Services
P.O. Box 2599
Raleigh, North Carolina 27602

NORTH DAKOTA
Department of Social Services
Capitol Building
Bismarck, North Dakota 58501

Catholic Family Services
Box 686
Fargo, North Dakota 58102

Lutheran Social Services of North Dakota
1325 11th Street South
Box 389
Fargo, North Dakota 58102

Children's Village
1721 South University Drive
Box 528
Fargo, North Dakota 58102

OHIO

Division of Social Services
Department of Public Welfare
Oak Street at Ninth
Columbus, Ohio 43215

Geauga County Department of Welfare
13281 Ravenna Road
Chardon, Ohio 44024

Montgomery County Children Services Board
3501 Merrimac Avenue
Dayton, Ohio 45405

Children Services of Richland County
50 Park Avenue East—4th Floor
Mansfield, Ohio 44902

Summit County Children Services Board
264 South Arlington Street
Akron, Ohio 44306

Children's Protective Service
Ohio Humane Society
2400 Reading Road
Cincinnati, Ohio 45215

Catholic Charities of Dayton
922 West Riverview Avenue
Dayton, Ohio 45407

Jewish Family Service
1175 College Avenue
Columbus, Ohio 43209

OKLAHOMA

Department of Institutions
Social and Rehabilitative Services
Sequoyah Memorial Office Building
Oklahoma City, Oklahoma 73125

OREGON

Children's Services Division
Department of Human Resources
Public Service Building
Salem, Oregon 97310

Appendix

Battered Child Committee
Department of Pediatrics
University of Oregon Medical School
3181 S.W. Sam Jackson Park Road
Portland, Oregon 97201

PENNSYLVANIA
Bureau of Child Welfare
Office of Children and Youth
State Department of Public Welfare
Harrisburg, Pennsylvania 17120

RHODE ISLAND
Rhode Island Department of Social and Rehabilitative Services
Child Welfare Services
600 New London Avenue
Cranston, Rhode Island 02920

SOUTH CAROLINA
State Department of Social Services
Box 1520
Columbia, South Carolina 29202

Connie Maxwell Children's Home
P.O. Box 1178
Greenwood, South Carolina 29646

SOUTH DAKOTA
Service Administration
State Department of Public Welfare
State Office Building
Pierre, South Dakota 57501

TENNESSEE
Department of Public Welfare
State Office Building
Nashville, Tennessee 37219

Children's Protective Agency
Humane Educational Society
212 North Highland Park Avenue
Chattanooga, Tennessee 37404

TEXAS
Texas State Department of Public Welfare
Division of Special Services
John H. Reagan Building
Austin, Texas 78701

UTAH
Bureau of Family and Children's Services
State Division of Family Services
231 East 4th South
Salt Lake City, Utah 84111

VERMONT
Division of Child Services
Department of Social Welfare
Montpelier, Vermont 05602

VIRGINIA
Bureau of Family and Children's Services
Division of General Welfare
State Department of Welfare and Institutions
429 South Belvidere Street
Richmond, Virginia 23220

WASHINGTON
Social Services Division
Department of Social and Health Services
P.O. Box 1788
Olympia, Washington 98504

WEST VIRGINIA
Division of Social Services
Department of Welfare
Charleston, West Virginia 25305

WISCONSIN
Division of Family Services
Department of Health and Social Service
1 West Wilson Street
Madison, Wisconsin 53702

WYOMING
Division of Public Assistance and Social Services
Department of Health and Social Services
State Office Building
Cheyenne, Wyoming 82001

BIBLIOGRAPHY

Bakan, D. *Slaughter of the Innocents.* San Francisco: Josey-Bass Inc., 1971.

Barta, R. A., Jr., and N. J. Smith. "Willful Trauma to Young Children." In *Clinical Pediatrics*, vol. 2, October 1963, 545–54.

Burt, R. A. "Protecting Children from Their Families and Themselves: State Laws and the Constitution." *Journal of Youth and Adolescence,* vol 1, 1971, 91–97.

Children's Division, American Humane Association. *Guidelines for Legislation to Protect the Battered Child.* Denver: American Humane Association, 1963.

Elmer, E. *Fifty Families Study: A Study of Abused and Neglected Children and Their Families.* Pittsburgh: University of Pittsburgh School of Medicine, 1965.

Fonta, V. J. *The Maltreated Child: The Maltreatment Syndrome in Children.* Springfield, Ill.: Charles C. Thomas, 1964.

Helfer, R. E., and C. H. Kempe. *The Battered Child.* Chicago: University of Chicago Press, 1968.

Helfer, R. E., and C. H. Kempe, Eds. *Helping the Battered Child and his Family.* Philadelphia: J. B. Lippincott, 1972.

National Council of Juvenile Court Judges. *Judges Look at Themselves.* A report by the National Council of Juvenile Court Judges, Chicago, 1965.

Sussman, F. B., and F. S. Baum. *Law of Juvenile Delinquency.* Dobbs Ferry, N.Y.: Oceana Publications, 1968.

Young, L. *Wednesday's Children: A Study of Child Neglect and Abuse.* New York: McGraw-Hill, 1964.